Dove Legend

Drawing by Barbara Howard

Richard Outram

Dove Legend
& Other Poems

The Porcupine's Quill

CANADIAN CATALOGUING IN PUBLICATION DATA

Outram, Richard, 1930–
Dove legend: & other poems

ISBN 0-88984-221-3

I. Title.

PS8529.U8D68 2001   C813'.54   C2001-930041-7
PR9199.3097D68 2001

Canadä

Published by The Porcupine's Quill,
68 Main Street, Erin, Ontario N0B 1T0.
Readied for press by John Metcalf; copy-edited by Doris Cowan.
Typeset in Bauer Bodoni, printed on Zephyr Antique laid,
and bound at The Porcupine's Quill Inc.

Represented in Canada by the Literary Press Group.
Trade orders are available from General Distribution Services.

We acknowledge the support of the Ontario Arts Council,
and the Canada Council for the Arts for our publishing program.
The financial support of the Government of Canada
through the Book Publishing Industry Development Program
is also gratefully acknowledged.

1   2   3   •   02   01

This book is for Barbara

She rests, beyond compare, beyond repose.
Between the armatures of darkness she has seen
light summoning the rose.

PART I

Eros Descending

Consolation of the Savant

This spike-mace-cased, treasure-burnished,
    marron conker of ratiocination is
        an adamant nut to crack,
            yes, but

my love's lucid, elusive damsel-ephemera,
    brilliant Imperfect in light-skeins of
        gossamer thought caught,
            is not.

Feats of Frailty

I can imagine you ardent, my absent Natasha;
your downy oxters, your roseate hinder parts:
et voilà! 'It's Master Rodney Oakhampton
at your service, Jack of Venereal Arts.'

And I can imagine the horny young bumpkin Adam,
salacious but gormless, tupping before the Fall
with libidinous scheming prelapsarian Evie;
mere child's play, folks, no problem at all.

I can imagine the sensual Garden, ripened, reeking,
seething with coiling and uncoiling phallic snakes
and voluptuous with great velvet, vulva-wet blossoms
in, of a lamb's tail, only two shakes.

Or I can imagine umpteen astonishing variations
of the Story; all naughty, all ending up with bed
and the whole damned Wagnerian Liebeslied. What
I can't imagine is getting it out of my head.

Sometimes I can even imagine that I can imagine
God imagining me in my carnal intemperate lust
for the animal consummation of the Imagination
imagining Her Creation, Natasha … but only just.

Late Love Poem

Well. Here we are. Where we have always been,
of course; and sometimes recognized as such.
I wonder that the cosmos can survive
the theme and variation of your touch.

Well, there you go, where we have never gone:
off course, but something understood at last.
I doubt that even God remembers, dear,
the paths that we have scrambled in the past.

Well this is it. At least we think it is,
or may have been, or may be at the close
of any narrative of passion and reprieve.
My God you are redemptive in repose!

Well. Just as well. The others never got
beyond the starting gate; and if they won
the velvet pisspot, with rosette, so what?
By God sweetheart you always jumped the gun!

Well that is that. Finito. QED.
Wrapped up in greaseproof paper. That's show biz:
'Styx nix hix pix.' Okay, I know it ain't
all over till it's over. Then it is.

Well, what the Hell. Or Heaven. Which is where
we came in Love and which is where we leave.
Earth to earth, the sure and certain earth,
earth Incorruptible. I shall not grieve.

Yackety Sax

The smallest mammal of our clime
weighs in at less than one thin dime.

How like the brightheart of a shrew,
battering, my love, are you,

the which has known in parlous heat
death by the violence of its beat.

A shrew must, foraging its fate,
consume each day its body's weight

and rage rapacious through each night.
It too secretes a venomed bite.

Sweet savage fever, to adore,
insatiable, an omnivore,

for should chance have two shrews confined,
they must become one of a kind

and I don't mind.
And I don't mind.

Scorn from the Throne

'We have no time for this twaddle!' Regina
Clarissima, Queen of the Soapsuds, snapped.

'Baleful ambassadors, kicking stiletto heels
in rococo ante-rooms, clutching their bulls;
boffins brandishing fascicle blackprints
of daft perpetual patent emotion machines;
bishops with schemes for the greater fleecing
of sheep to the glory of indigent Mammon;
flogging rear-admirals spoiling to pillage
the fabulous innocent Sacrosanct Islands.

'No! By our rub-a-dub tub-reddened Rood, no!

'There are lithe condemned lovers entwined
in our carnal Queendom's voluptuous bolsters
gasping for royal pardon, grasping at bubbles,
glair spectra of brightness broadcast aloft
in ephemeral spirals, in fleet iridescent
yet-to-be-captured constellations and comets
of quivering globular prisms that vanish,
alas, in the quick blink of our kindled
cockatrice-boast world like burst eyeballs
under the understood once-sunburst sun!'

Diapason in *Thimble Theatre*

Some marriages, after Byzantine negotiations, are arranged.
Some poleaxed lovers swear their trothplight on the spot.
Some marriages, so we are informed, are made in Heaven.
And some marriages rather evidently are not.

But surely one of the least congruous of nuptials
ever to have been solemnized under the blanched moon
was the decorous matrimony of George Weintraub Geezil,
widower, to the sometime parish spinster, Alice the Goon.

History does not record the details of their courtship.
There are those who conjecture, that Geezil took off his hat
and knelt, when he proposed. On the other hand, many
are prepared to believe in bizarreries, but not that.

The ceremony itself is a matter of vestry record.
The bride was given away by Ludwig Wittgenstein.
A tearful Olive was her bridesmaid. Rough-house hosted
the saturnalian reception. From Cana came the wine.

Fie! A plague upon you, who would, prurient, follow after
the radiant couple, beyond the closed bridal-chamber door!
Did Geezil cradle Alice, or Alice Geezil? O whatever rapture
connubial was theirs is privy, and secret evermore.

And was their union steadfast as the constellations?
Or fraught with discord? Again, history does not relate:
and not just because Elzie Crisler Segar put aside his pen
to give up the ghost, in nineteen thirty-eight.

Clio belaboured does not utter in these matters.

Inquire of Hymen, or Erato, as every schoolboy knows,
on love's ingenious carnalities: but none shall tell
the stricken mysteries of Souls that juxtapose.

Drama

The Villain's stove-pipe hat spewed thick black smoke;
his moustache bristled in red rage; he hissed and spat
invective, threat; his black cloak writhed. To no avail.

The Maid remained a virgin. To her cornflower-blue-eyed,
flaxen-tressed, sweet-rosebud-lipped and infinite chagrin.
The mortgage was foreclosed. Ma went to the poor-farm.

The stalwart Hero had been pinked, a paltry scratch:
by vile contrivance the blade's tip had been tainted.
He staggered downstage and collapsed. The curtain rose.

The flesh, the flesh dissembles. And our death becomes us.

The Gift

He gave to his love, for her twenty-first birthday,
an erotic print, from Jodhpur Rajasthan, circa 1820.

In the Indian night, the sky hovered above them
is roiled blue-black, with curious serpentine
squiggles of dull yellow, suggesting script.

Within the pavilion, sequestered from prying eyes
by luxurious vegetation, the virile young prince,
kneeling, has entered his carefully shaved
concubine from behind. She is shewn in profile.

And she is as taut, as flexible to his desire,
as the recurved bow he bends, of sinew and horn,
above her compliant spine. When his loosed shaft
pierces the gold pard, furtive, come down to drink
at the alabaster ghat, then the world will end.

Evidence in the Garden

While the beast is gentled,
Adam, randy man,
Slip into her traces
Where you can;

Leave her sleeping body,
Silvered in the stream
Where she has been savaged,
Dark with dream;

Leave the moon-flecked leopard
Tangled in the tree
Gleamed above her, keeping
What must be,

Until the sun is risen
And the trampled field
Of husbandry and bloodstain
Is revealed:

Then innocent of morning,
The fallen light unfurled,
Slip into the fallow
Habitable world.

Generation

Susanna is having her bath.
Lovingly she laves.
Pious elders have gathered round
to watch. They are her slaves.

One of them steps on the soap
and breaks his scrawny neck.
Nobody pays the least heed.
At Susanna's slightest beck,

they proffer exotic unguent;
at Susanna's faintest call,
they undulate like stroked fronds.
They are in elders' thrall.

Susanna soaps deftly up,
Susanna soaps deftly down,
Susanna soaps covert in between.
Joakim's out of town.

Seraphim, bending, choir!
Cherubim give glad shout!
At last at last from the lapis tank,
Susanna is stepping out!

Pearls of her mist emprism
the godly sun's rough rays;
the elders breathe in unison
fleet orisons of praise,

---

to see where she lifts her arms
to towel her cascade hair,
sweet martyrdom incarnate: flushed,
Susanna is standing bare,

and bending forward to comb,
permitting the languorous breeze
unthinkable privilege. About
the courtyard are many trees;

and hid by the mastic bole,
or under the evergreen oak,
a swart tormented Daniel skulks,
wrapped in his Judgement cloak.

'Alarum, O Israel!
Assemble, all Moses' kind!
Let lewdest elders suffer! O
my people, are you blind?'

And Daniel shall tell the tale.
And righteous shall be his wrath,
that pious elders may nevermore
see Susanna in the bath.

Eros Incarnate

Beyond the reach
Of any tether,
Long desperate
For other weather,
Bestowed, pathetic,
Inhuman, given,
As Love informs us
We are driven;
Erase the halo
Round her head;
My Love waits, naked,
On our bed:
My Love, our Love;
And, once, again,
The sacred proved
By the profane,
What wound, what waters
Bathe her side,
What wells of brightness
Break my Bride,
That such precise
Commands of Grace
Grow myriad
In time and place,
As Sacrament
Embodied there;
What more shall mortal
Body bear?

———

Magdalena Enamoured

As in some fragile vessel put to sea,
which wayward winds have driven far from shore
and all the haven she has set in store,
against the strictures of mortality;

the currents hurrying her craft along
no helm can temper, nor true chart depict,
nor rose correct where she is derelict
in Sirens' recapitulated song;

yet as she turns toward the very waves
that thrust her through profundities of force
upon her boundless undetermined course,
the subtle ways in which she misbehaves

will order all the elements to move
in startled indirection to her love.

Ever

After, lying watching clouds,
hurrying and low,
are we two no longer one?
It seems so.

Whatever, dear heart, do you make,
secret in your sleep,
of my insinuated hand?
It will keep.

Then let this moment, gentled, be
ephemeral as thought,
or disembodied love. It is.
And is not.

On Our Anniversary

When these dark lovely things we do
have been exhausted and run through
by night, to prove our bodies true

to one another in their way,
before we come to face the day
let us embrace again, who may

(yet in our kindled brightness blind
to brightness) in this fire find
another body come to mind,

the conflagration of a Man
Immortal in his blazing span
and provenance: and if we can,

embodied, neither graced nor lured,
who have this Phoenix-flame endured,
arise again by Love assured.

Caress

Lifting her gaze, by chance
bemused,
and in a naked glance
recognizing her own,

Barbara

who has grown
roses in winter, knew me
burdened,
and gave them to me.

The Deaths of Animals

Lux est umbra Dei

Or such is our surmise.

I feel your sleeping pulse
incessantly repeat
again – again – again –
strangely here, my blood
neither boils nor chills;
not ichor-altered so,
it neither thrills nor sings,
despite what poets say,

but goes its way
on mortal roundabout
of man and burnished beast,
with no brass ring,
no fatal lovely prize,
no glittering single thing.
If once we were at least
or most beyond all doubt,
if we could choose

to make up all we lose
upon the given swings,
now knowing what we know
of what blood spills,
I do not think we would
take anything in vain,
untroubled in this beat:
or else – or else – or else.

Or have it otherwise.

PART II

Around & About the Toronto Islands

Hanlan's as Lunatic Venue

The cast-iron-tree-trunk-stanchioned dance pavilion,
scene of my sometime bitter-sweet late adolescent lusts,
is long since gone. They did frown, the godly Puritans,

on carnal pleasures: bull-mastiffs baiting blinded bears
and suchlike rough-and-tumble sport; or quick knee-tremblers
that might to lewdness of the dance rude clodpolls lead.

I watched one bloodsun morning while a small hanged man
was cut down from a gibbet willow. And in that selfsame tree
observed a recent migrant rarity, a yellow-breasted chat.

It did not sing of *autres moeurs*. Oh no. It kept no scuzzy
developers awake. It did not give, gold bird in golden bush
of reminiscent moons. Like nothing else on Hanlan's Point.

29

Together on Gibraltar Point

Like buoyed toys, white gulls ride
high on the long swells:
they are aligned into the west wind,
and slant evening light strikes
their breasts ruddy on slate water.
They seem decoys, carved from grained light.

As we, attendant, may well be, if not yet
God's spies, God's decoys; set
out in the hope, however faint,
that somehow betimes a migrant truth
will appear; to circle, uncertain,
hover perhaps, and reassured settle

to whatever construction or resolution
of life or of death.

Picnic Table

It is a given construction, it is all geometry
in the full welter of midsummer's green.

As is its exact shadow cast on the cropped grass;
it shortens and lengthens and pivots with the sun.

Its top is a palimpsest, scrawled and crude-carved
by the hopeful, the lustful, the bored, the bereaved.

And the blasphemous: those who despoil whatever
is blessed, immersed in their private madness.

Who shall number the numberless, layer on layer
of slathered paint, weathered to cobalt-viridian?

It is no small thing, it is an amenity, civilizations
rise and fall and are reckoned by such matters.

And in the autumn it will be stacked with its kind,
in the lee of a yellow willow, in a long row,

each with its forefeet planted upon the canted back
of the next like a line of great beasts breeding

against the season, the coming of certain winter.

Time and Again on Olympic

Alone at last, one half of one, or less,
with the profligate fly, all day buzz buzz
in the mind, casting the rank green tangle
of nondescript Paradise Island, alone, alone.

How long, O Lord, how long in abundance, after
the foretold passing over the warped horizon
must we then wait, painstakingly watching
the restless unaltered water, always annealed,

for what might or might not befall, O for what
might or might not be an Ark's recollected wake?

Halfway Along

We have admired the plumped-up pillars bowed
like calyx-tubes of pomegranate flowers,
the balusters within the balustrades that span
the hump-backed bridge, almost from infancy.

And have in childhood peered between them down
upon the noonblaze of Long Pond and watched
great coin-sheathed carp upon occasion rise
to bask above the pollen-columned depths.

We do thank Man for tourmaline-green pleached
limes; kempt beds of salvia, that 'Bids
the rash gazer wipe his eye'; the old-
rose-velvet nicotine that floods the dusk.

Then there is Centreville ... well, sparrow-fart!
We have good reason to be thankful for
the spray that splays and falls and, levelled, brims
to spill us ragged light in bright cascade,

hard by the misremembered cedar maze.
Not mighty, no; 'but not without a plan'
(beware, dear heart, of emendation!). Everywhere
is Centre, friend: 'presume not God to scan'.

Vessel

(aboard the *Cayuga*)

The distant, bruised horizon line
and an exact steel-wire guy
have intersected to define,
so far as one can judge by eye,

an angle seen to fluctuate
through only three or four degrees,
exhibiting our steady rate
of passage over placid seas

upon a constant bearing. Aft,
the undulation of our wake
is jostling the smaller craft,
diverging furrows through the lake.

We have lost sight of land at last.
To starboard, leaving us amazed
by all similitude, a vast
bright-hatching image-sun is blazed.

The diesels throbbed below us, come
in endless repetition, lull
us from our senses: we are numb,
the creatures of our tremored hull,

where we are silenced and constrained
within this constancy: we feel
ourselves persist in the sustained
reverberation of the steel.

You, beside me, let your head
fall on my shoulder in a way
familiar to us from our bed.
I watch the vectored circles play,

which, since we left, have never slept
upon the trembled silver disc
of water in the bucket kept,
that we should be the less at risk,

against all unexpected fire.
And deeply moved, I see repeat,
absolved here even of desire,
the measured, certain, fluent beat

that Love will trouble once again
and vulnerable will persist:
the little pulse along the vein
half hidden in your inner wrist.

Sojourn on Snake Island

How much time must be spent, friend, in my trying to tell you?
That the lake water wallops the pilings and never in vain;
that the heat-shimmer over the gravel is pure distortion.
You would number the numberless midges again and again?

Well now, how about ten, say, to the eighty-seventh power:
a winsome, a lose-some number, and one you can take to heart
both for motes and for light-years. And at least it is better
than nothing at all: shall we say, it will do for a start?

Look I'm trying to tell you please don't walk away in a tizzy
from a prolix clean-shaven loon who has been around eftsoons.
It takes precious time for the brass ring to oxidize a patina;
there are always free rides and lunches on languorous afternoons.

We will weave here and now from the ravelled thread of our story
and the fragile strand of our discourse a tissue of fabulous lies,
such that the raddled old Emperor's oldest clothes be bespoken
again, as raiment for heavenly bodies. Look through glass eyes!

Tutelary Abroad on the Boardwalk

The shortest distance between two points
is not always a dead straight line, old Joe
Sobersides, but a given segment, sometimes,
of this diminishing-into-the-distance curve.

And the longest lapse between two instants
is seldom eternity, young Jack Hickathrift:
consider the stolid abeyance between the arrival
of humdrum waves, breaking one after another.

To be here on the boardwalk, walking *hey presto!*
into the spring light while the lake water knocks
at the bedrock of all possible islands is –
hiccius doccius! – to be in the evident present

of toing and froing, of celebration, of harlequin
spinnakers coursing tatterdemalion clouds;
of lightning above the wiry horizon rebounding
like Mjölnar into the grasp of absent, alas, Thor.

Island Residents

We have heard complaint elaborated endlessly:
that they are raucous, as individuals or in concert;
that they are disrespectful of appointed authority;
that they are profligate, indiscriminate breeders;
that they are by nature unclean – in fact, lousy!

That they are squatters, fly-by-nights that pay
sweet nothing for slum-homes on public lands,
which are ramshackle, badly cobbled, jerry-built,
unsanitary, scantling firetraps that fail
to meet the city's stringent building codes;

and that their jostling young are raised unschooled
and barefoot; that their elders are mad-eyed,
rapacious, belligerent and dangerous to press;
that they contribute nought to Metro's weal;

is – each and every charge, friends, – true!
Inarguably true; demonstrably the case.
And one might add, they are incontinent as well;
and whiten their surrounds with lengthened streaks
of chalky, nacreous-slimed shite.

Yet strangely, the black-crowned night herons
have this season quit the sanctuary of Mugg's
Island, have abandoned Blockhouse Bay, for other,
greener, lofted heronries upon the man-made spit;
and of entirely their own inscrutable volition.

The Islanders on Ward's and on Algonquin, however
(to this you had best accustom yourselves, friends),
say of them what you will, are there to stay.

Turner Reports of the Storm's Subsidence

All yesterday I watched the light – ah, you were not
There – warped pale glass-green – the slant sun shot

Through high rolled-over waves about to break
In heaving ranks along the outraged lake

And thundering down attempt once more to knock
The living Daemon from the adamantine rock –

And then in turmoil churned glass-green again I saw
Th'reluctant waves – dark mauve-glass-green – withdraw.

Shade on Ward's
(for Arrow)

Past the stench-pipe,
down the tiles,
goes Grimalkin;
in her wiles

insidious
as darkling fog.
On the prowl
is Egypt mog,

feral, mortal,
single-bent:
all copulation
her intent.

Who gainsays her?
Not you, not I.
The curs of Hell
give tongue to hie

our sleeping souls
to perished earth
& nine-lived death
& virgin's birth.

Tower across the Water

She foresees:

when the first night migrant batters
death to very death against
the aloft goldglass façade and drops
moteblood through blooded cusps
to arisen earth no fires unfold
no chasm below opens enraged
to receive her no moment is closed.

None.

And when the last mirror flashes
against the several blade not even
the instant Angel, twinned,
shall escape unscathed.

Ever.

Meet Stance at the Eastern Gap

The lightfall is ascending!
The sky is marine green!
The lake is tufted with white cloud!
Whatever can this mean?

Has this too too solid earth
flipped? O no: instead,
I, haphazard Islander,
am standing on my head.

Trillium

Throughout the solar day,
as on a molten track,
the ferry crosses the bay.
Then the ferry crosses back.

When it appears she must
bear down on and collide
with some free sail, we trust
perspective to provide

that they shall pass unscathed,
still steadfast in our sight.
Here, where the bay is bathed
in shuddered summer light

she seems, from our island view,
like some expensive toy.
This world, not quite askew,
is persistent to deploy

such vessels, whereby we
may come, perhaps, to learn
what regimens must be,
to set forth and return

at an appointed hour.
The water, mirror-flat,
conveys her wake to scour
the shore. And we know that

her Master will decline
all error or surmise
whose passengers, supine,
lay obols on their eyes.

PART III

Abstract Memoir

At Close of Eve

Titania dreams: I tiptoe down before the winter dawn.
Here, left half-peeled, half-eaten, liver-spotted, this
banana lies, its splayed fronds blackened overnight,
becoming in the pewter gloom some problematic bat,
dilapidated on the azure countertop.

                                                  My aproned aunt
Kathleen, who did not marry, by despair dismayed,
once swatted one before my dazzled eyes: she flailed
the summer-kitchen corn broom wildly to and forth,
fro and back, with all her slight might mightily until,
more by beginner's luck than jousting grace, at last
she caught it square and (destinies considered) fair
in sweet mid-arc perfection of its flight:

                                                         O where
it crumpled, fell, and twitching, chittering like shrill
spilled radio and bleeding from its wizard's snout,
it died. I did, if unencumbered then, and some pale
daybreaks natheless still do, disbelieve – for all
your vaunted heartbreak-kindness, regal Oberon.

Narcissus

A custom, ever since childhood;
often, just following Advent,
when winter seems endless.

Having begun to sprout, lying
every-which-way, to the light,
now potted, some shoots are canted
like green-billed ducks thrusting
back over parchment bodies;
some curve like tusks, wicked,
from lapped, fine, cuticle sheaths;
one, a minute green fuse to
a comic-strip anarchist's bomb.

We have planted them chock-a-block,
squat brown chubs of bulbs
nestled in smooth, glacier-tumbled
pebbles older even than they.
Regarded, they bring to mind
a Japanese family tub; a jammed
nest of grotesque fledglings;
damned souls writhing in some
mediaeval depiction of Hell
and its jostled torments.

As we were advised, they sat
a week in a cold, dark place,
that their first thrust be downward
expended, into a thick meshing
of blind white rootlets, solid
lest they lift upwards too swiftly
their vigorous several stalks:

too swiftly, too slender, too tall;
to topple thereafter under
the burden of subsequent blossom.

Thirsty, requiring a daily
top-up of clear water,
in no time it seems they become
all vertical blades, trembled,
a marvellous delicate coppice
of thin green flames, wavering.
That they ascend straitly,
we turn them each morning,
for they reach to the window.

Until on entering the room
of an evening, we find them,
drenched in the lamplight, there,
a radiant haze of white blossom,
everything promised, themselves.
And we are drenched also, caught
unawares and stricken, bewildered
with scent so empowered, pervasive;
a summons extended to death
and to life in the natural realms;
and out of our fecund darkness
a beckoning from us of passionate
faces and gestures and lost places,
antiquities, memories and further,
stranger, forever archaic selves.

Stage Crew

Remember how, with those reluctant gangs
Of punks and drunks and aesthetes in blue jeans
And brittle British thespians and thugs
And innocents and sods and ex-Marines,
We filled the slipshod nights by daft degrees
With intricate, fantastical machines

To hold a gimcrack mirror up to Art?
O darkly, darkly, honest souls asleep,
Dreamless we watched the painted cities rise,
The canvas worlds collapsed into a heap.
A house of cards, a rhythmless quick flux
That might make Job or Heraclitus weep

Contained us handsomely; what could we learn,
Coming to grips (you will forgive the pun)
With that ménage, those dear wild bootless men,
As best we could? When all was said and done
They were the stuff, the burden of the Love
That we had need to find. As one by one

They pass like ribald mummers through the mind
I find for each his legend and event:
Stefen, who froze his penis in the Alps,
Or Pat, who burned his captain in his tent,
Or Vernon, who had slept with movie queens.
An endless ragged masque, they came and went

From slums or public schools or prison camps
To Thules or Bermudas or disgrace.
But for a spell we worked and cursed and fought
And laughed with them: they were that motley race
Wherein we learned to watch for God's delight,
Framed, fleetingly, within a human face.

Neighbour

Listen! Mad Anne is angry! Backyards away, we catch
Scraps of vituperation; a variegated hatch
Of florid four-letter oaths; sobs in a batch;

Some of it makes sense. Iniquitous to relate,
Children hurry to mock her, watching her fulminate.
No one has heard her, ever, rail against God; or Fate;

Or the brute drunk that she lives with, or his carved cur;
Or the tom with the head like a furred boot, that adopted her
To provide, on her good days, for her, magniloquent purr.

She has not seemingly cursed, through all of her arid years
Among us as friend and neighbour, however reduced to tears,
Our casual turned backs, the least of her fears:

No, no: she will stop, of a sudden, enraged at the concrete!
At a shard! A shadow! A diamond reflection before her feet!
Having been pierced terribly, once, by the too discrete.

My Grandmother

Before she died possessed a sphere
Of glass set in a burnished base
Of what she said was ebon wood:
When it was taken from its place

Beside the Bible by her bed
And gently shaken upside down
And then replaced, we watched a slow
Snowstorm smothering a town,

Bereft of all inhabitants,
With heavy sedimental flakes
Through liquid silence. Wherewith death
Was demonstrated for our sakes.

As silently, all afternoon,
Beneath a seamless sky, a slight
Breeze is broadcasting a drift,
From some tall poplar out of sight,

Of bits of light-entangled lint
Sent slantwise through the crystal air,
Conveying multitudes of seed,
Each burdened with, encoded there,

A living phenotypal tree,
The replication of its kind.
By dusk the lawn is blanketed.
As recompense, she used to find

A text for each of us to read
Aloud to her. Ezekiel's wheel
Rolled murderous above her bed.
Sweet Jesus, teach us what is real!

Gramp

His sight began to fail
when I was still a child.
They came to teach him Braille,
but he was far too old,
cantankerous, and wild
to do as he was told,

as usual. But still,
considering his age,
he worked at Moon, until
he tore the dimpled cards
to shreds in frustrate rage
one April morning. Yards,

not miles, of darkness stretched
before him at the worst,
he reckoned. And we fetched
and carried; and he tried
to cope; and quit and cursed
the fickle light and died.

I, too young back then
to mourn or understand
the freighted lives of men,
or death as a relief
and not dark contraband,
who had not suffered grief,

now tender him good night:
remembering the glare
of hammered waterlight
reflected in his eyes,
his perfect patience where
a rainbow trout might rise.

Barbed Wire

Consists of two tight-twisted, separate strands
Conjoined as one: and not unlike, in fact,
Our own familiar silver wedding bands,
Though these are loosely woven, inexact,

With wide interstices, so that each makes
A circle of ellipses. Tightly caught
At random intervals, two little snakes
Of wire are crimped into a snaggled knot,

That four short ends, sharp bevel-cut, present
Unsheathed ingenious fangs. And when in place,
Stretched taut, or strewn in loose coils, may prevent
The passage through some designated space

Of beast, or man. You got used to the stench;
The mud was worse than being under fire,
My father said. A detail left the trench
At night, to get the dead back from the wire,

And no one volunteered. They stood, to view
Our brief exchange of rings and vows, for both
Our fathers had survived that war: and knew
Of death, and bright entanglement, and troth.

Presence

It may be that despite time I have heard,
or overheard, someone I never knew
in person, having listened deeply stirred
by strange familiarity where you

are singing softly to yourself, bemused
and vulnerable, without conscious choice,
some phrase of recollected song she used
to cherish you in childhood, and your voice

that I seem always to have loved and known
is yours and more than yours: I only know
that we are gathered by our loves, as we have grown
into our love, and that it might be so.

Bank Swallow
(In memory of F.L.B.)

Sudden, in an instant where the wind,
the brief momentum of her upward arc,
blade-winged, and constant gravity resolve,
I see her frozen, motionless, a spark

of life suspended perfectly before
the primitive ignition of the sun
that leaves me dazzled, following her flight;
and am reminded how, when all is done

and left unsaid of death, we may remain
amazed in vision: knife-swift, she is gone
to jagged brightness in between the spruce
that cast their jagged shadow on the lawn.

Remembrance of Betty E.

It is certainly one strange kettle of fish, we were all agreed,
sitting around the table, chatting. As if it had all been planned,
the cosmos, it seems, unless it bursts first, is, like some vast
barrage balloon gone bonkers, continuing infinitely to expand;
and then it may, or again it may not, completely collapse back
to a pointless, unthinkably dense mote, incomprehensibly bland;
also, some boffins are starting to talk as if the whole boiling
is a loony tune being played by a one-man band.

And the heat-death of our own insignificant sun is icumin in,
a few tens of millions of years ahead; not a bad one-night stand
for the likes of us zany players, since according to Bishop Ussher
the Creation in every detail occurred in exactly 4004 BC ... and
as you pointed out (if we hadn't all loved you already, Betty,
we must have forever after!) a half-hour earlier in Newfoundland.

Chance Encounter

It takes a moment, then
I resurrect your name.
We knew each other when
at college we were friends,
who started on the same
path for different ends

and have not met for years.
Of course we stop to talk.
Now neither of us fears
the other, I suppose.
Our smiling wives take stock
of one another's clothes.

You too are going grey,
and thickening, and like me
are careful not to say
those things that might parade
old wounds or loves. I see
you wear a hearing aid.

We mention so-and-so,
and good old what's-his-face,
and probably both know
what each has left unsaid
of triumphs or disgrace:
a lot of them are dead,

or best forgotten. Well,
life, we agree, is strange;
and we must lunch, we tell
each other, for a start;
shake hands, do not exchange
our addresses, and part.

And you will never know
how one of your askew
remarks once pierced me so,
all subsequent event
swerved: not that I knew
for certain what you meant.

Night Vision
(for Ernest)

On watch, we had to learn
How, if we would discern
Out of the heaving swarm
Of darkened waters, form,
That accident might loom
Specific from the gloom,
Or a faint prick of light
Hint at the bound of night,
To train our every glance
Somehow just askance.

And could not value more
That adumbrated shore,
The landfall that not quite
Burns at the verge of sight.

But Man may come to prove
Vision, Logos, Love,
Impregnate; the behest
Modalities that best
Enhance our prayer to be
Where reason holds that we,
Blind creatures that we are
Before our sun, our star
Searing in its sway,
Shall see by day.

Fifty-seven Years of Infinity

Rainbow Barber Shop, Yonge Street, 1936

Confronted by the infinite, the imaged
Recession of my selves
With multiples of multicoloured unguents
And tonics on sloped shelves,

That, alternating front and back forever
In upward curving thrust,
Resigned this mirrored mirrored world for somewhere,
As it somehow must,

I made a swift propitiating gesture
Upon the swivelled chair
That had a child's seat set across the armrests,
Then sat immobile there,

Lest I should slip into that sly ascension:
Until, at last deemed done,
I clambered down, wet-combed, perfumed, diminished
But once more one.

Elevator, 1993

So smooth is my silent progress it seems to be stasis;
a single punctilious light warns me that I am falling.

And there is, it appears, an infinite number of me
in this dim-lit, decorous, multiple-mirrored box:

we reach, in a slight and slightly ascending curve
on either interim hand in this hutch of reflections,

my self and this given obsequious host so prolonged,
to the limit of human vision. Love, this is not life.

I smile, thus embarrassed; and am mocked in an instant
declension of selfhood where I am indeed become verb,

save there is no other, no saving second person wherein
I may be beside myself, bereft in delight or heartbreak.

And this is not death. We have faith in closeted death,
a faith garnered at length from the evidence of things

seen in this world of which we are all celebrants. Hell
('... the inability to love') is prefigured however:

in this imaged durance, this seamless abeyance attended
by serried selves waiting for doors perhaps to open.

Northumbria

Lindisfarne Priory
(Holy Island, October 1994)

It is the long dark waves and their serpentine ways of cresting,
collapsing at last into cobalt slather; and the unthinkable rage
of late sun catching the chip of some glittered distant vessel,
making for somewhere for some reason, that brings the page

to mind: the meanders of faded azure, and gold, and delicate rose;
and the intricate margins with beaked creatures entwined, exact;
and the aureoled wingèd man, lion, calf and the wing that is eagle,
each bearing a book. Only the one rainbow arch is intact

where, as from the Beginning and all uncomprehended beginnings,
to the four or however-many-reckoned quarters of the unknown
and meantime irreconciled teeming world the intransigent Word,
we are told, has gone forth forever parlous, the winds have blown

harum-scarum over the coney-riddled, marram-tufted dunes,
over the staggered wracklines where, at present, one must walk
through the fierce pink, raw orange, garish yellow, unnatural green
and once-white plastic trashed on oil-blackened rock.

Gertrude Jekyll's Lindisfarne Castle Garden

So patterned it looks from above, as a migrant bird
might view it, or Icarus, or latterly man aloft,
like a skewed micro-chip fallen on ochre baize
dotted with placid sheep. It may be, that a soft

answer turneth wrath: when the terrible Danes
came the Christians fled. On three sides, high
limestone walls ward off the levelling gales;
Hudson lowered the south wall, to descry,

framed from the garden bench, his castle's heights.
On the crazed stone I watched one October day
the '... thin as a curve, a muscled ribbon,' uncoiled
and recoiled spring of a tawny weasel at play,

time and again in spasmodic savage attack
slashing a hollyhock head. One never knows:
plagued by a larval worm that may fatten deep
in the skull, sometimes a stoat or stricken weasel goes

berserk, indiscriminate mad, all incarnate rage.
The western rose border, after some sixty years,
suffered a soil sickness; the new roses did not
prosper, and couch grass took hold. Terror's arrears

will be paid in full, we are warned by those who recall
another implicate Garden; who reckon that God is just.
The whole show is owned now, and has been of course
managed since sixty-eight, by the National Trust.

Otters' Eyes

'… twitch and cry Love.'

Considering that it was
a farmhouse B&B,
and in the Cheviots,
it came as no surprise
when on arrival we
were greeted by a mask,
a vulpine, wry grimace
set with gemstone eyes,
beside the lintel, placed
to face the paying guest.

But neither of us saw,
or not until the next
morning, as we left
after our night's rest,
opposite the door,
an otter's snarling head
and under it two webbed
paws, the rear and fore,
spiked together, crossed.

And, curious, we asked.
'Oh, dear me, no, oh dear,
not at Otterburn; oh no,
there are no otters now
at Otterburn. Long gone.'
the Wooler baker said,

65

'... a military base, and
nowadays, well, sir,
you wouldn't want to know
the place; not nowadays.'

And there was a text
on our bedroom wall
in glazed lustreware;
it was mounted next
the mirror. I recall
what it said here:

*'But man dieth,
and wasteth away:
yea, man giveth
up the Ghost, and
where is he?'*

There must have been,
in former times,
a thriving taxidermy
trade: that stocked
wholesale supplies
in crafted glass
of otters' eyes
and graded them
by colour, size,
and one would pay,
back then as now,
for quality, excess
somehow ...

———

God knows,
the river otter
put to rout
the salmon and
incorrigibly ate
the rose-mole-
stippled trout
and sorely tried
the syndicate;
that wasn't on.

Long gone, long
gone. But once,
one gathers by
the evidence
of things unseen
here nowadays,
it was you see,
and must be still,
in many ways
a coveted and rare
delight to be
in at the kill.

House Plant

It was moss green,
in a biscuit pot,
on the brilliant sill.
Now it is not

the flourishing forth
we once thought
light to unlearn,
chance to allot

to love.

Now it is dust;
the one selfsame
at long last no
body of blame:

lest death let slip
its dusty name,
lest there be no end
to the late game

of love.

A Christ-Cross-Row

The wandering earth herself may be
Only a sudden flaming word,
In clanging space a moment heard,
Troubling the endless reverie.

– from 'Crossways' (1889), W.B. Yeats

After all has been said and done, my dear,
Before silence falls on our wandering earth,
Claiming, reclaiming a mortal Creature,
Damping all clanging space in the troubled,
Endless reverie where we shared a sudden
Flaming word, let us together consider,
Graced as we have been beyond our deserts,
How much has been spoken despite ourselves.
'In the beginning ...' Well, we have uttered
Justice, a delicate balance imperilled.
Knowledge, outwitting our feral rote.
Love which passeth even eros and agape.
Mercy, mercy! For we torture children.
Nothing: for 'Man has created death.'
O for the mute rapture of adoration.
Pity, coursed in our chartered streets.
Quality, for we avowed '... for better for worse'
Reverence, rarely perhaps, sometimes for life.
Sanity seldom, but never an ass's carrot.
Truth, strangest of all our estranged relations.
Utterance then: our wellspring of being human.
'Verily, I say unto you ...' Let it be said:
We are aware, this is a shortlist of numberless
Xenia we have been proffered, we transient,
Yearning, loquacious guests, of a sum numbered
Zero perhaps, yet numbering everything, Love.

PART IV

Tradecraft

Tradecraft

Goes with the territory, fireman (Save my Babe!)
which ain't, we are advised, the bleeding map.
Ask any pavement artist in the sanguine field:
none does offend. All my own work, I can ask one
condign in bastardy to tell me who I am, but not
on pain of suffering a fate far worse than life
(lace-curtain jobs are not for your timid souls)
demand a candid answer, daughter, to thy quis
custodiet ... it's Ms Fallacious on the blower
for you, Dad, expressing sympathy. Let's not
forget the possible improbable in art, or craft,
in an election year. Get thee glass eyes.

Wrangler, wrangler, where have you been?
I've been engrossed in what meaning might mean.
Wrangler, wrangler, what did you there?
I deciphered a little fact from Dzerzhinsky Square.

It's still a jungle out there, Evie baby; he/
she had devised, however, found, or been vouchsafed
the perfect drop: a burly guardsman's busby,
housing each evening a murmuration of stares,
directly in front of palatial Buckingham Palace,
folks; also the ideal fall-back: Home Sweet Home,
with a hunk of Mom's how-do-you-like-them-rotten-
disbranched-apples pie left simmering on the hob,
say cheese; they may be late about this business.
For there is conjuring abroad, no less no more.

Listener, listener, where have you been?
I've been in the back room for what I can glean.
Listener, listener, what did you there?

I gathered a little fact out of the blare.

Having befriended a scrumpy-hound, gone pong,
dossed down rough on the Embankment overnight,
a genuine piss-artist, ex-BBC, in drag,
who in the bitter morning was revealed to be
one of the lesser deities, now into tares,
the ritual ablutions and the staff canteen,
he had been granted a miraculous four-piece
Holy City suit that rendered him invisible.
In which he could tail assets back and forth
forever without backup; and could not for love
hee-haw! nor money hee-haw! himself be tailed.

Housekeeper, housekeeper, where have you been?
I've been on a paper chase serving the Queen.
Housekeeper, housekeeper, what did you there?
I enabled a little fact to split a hair.

He quailed in his own presence, and had come
to obviate all contact with his mirrored eye;
in the mysterious West despite his better self
embraced a martial art the juju master deemed
so formy-dabluh, with rosette and jaded belt,
that like old Stompin' Tennessee Tom Yahweh
it cannot be named, lest Cosmos self-destruct.
And qualified as lethal weapon, Mark whatever
X. Was designated henceforth simple minder and
best British baby-sitter. Registry, who knows
when one is dead and when one lives, was chuffed.

Flutterer, flutterer, where have you been?
I've been in a snarl with my silken machine.
Flutterer, flutterer, what did you there?

I sifted for fictions, fact being rare.

Well, junk indeed; but Waldorf, would you buy
a rusted, used and long discarded sunbeam
flivver from this con-man much dismissed? Age
should bring you Nunc *(bibendum est)* to some
late understanding of this common age of fools.

Th'insurance once laid on, the kickshaw laced,
the nasty capsule by tame fangmonger set hid
in the back molar, the salvific coup disguised
as a swig of Geritol, this is revealed as naught.
Egregious Ludwig laid it down, misunderstood:
all that is necessary strictly is to silent fall
never to speake againe. For nothing *will* come
of nothing (voices, ranting, off) O mad bon moT.
Chancery is said to be rethinking the whole
vexed expensive question of garrulous seniors.

Gorilla, gorilla, where have you been?
I've been up to Lubianka to play it obscene.
Gorilla, gorilla, what did you there?
I sweated a little fact out of its lair.

What can man disregard? We have not learned;
the history of Buncombe County still not writ
and having rote moves on to dusty wawl and cry.
The Antichrist, or at least *their* Antichrist
(with Casement at Iquitos, for starters, chum),
if seldom oracular in hallways and hullabaloo
of smoke and mirrors, recks and reveals thuswise:
when invoking the inessential need to know, for
the censor there is no repeat no discernible diff-
erence whatsolutely abever between God's anagogic

75

disinformation and for-Your-eyes-only. This is
classified Bottom Secret and shredded after death.

Coat trailer, coat trailer, where have you been?
I've been masquerading to see if you're keen.
Coat trailer, coat trailer, what did you there?
I honeyed a little fact for a Red Bear.

Put paid to persiflage, stout Watson, kindly lend
your strict attention to the matter, one will ask
grave questions later. Now of lendings learn
(see Fawn: *On Anticryptic and Procryptic Habit*);
Jake was trained and made, not born chameleon.
There is, so it would seem, a bloody proclamation
always to escape. One look for usual shoes.
Your issue anorak reverses; the swift switch,
Dodger, of titfers, Bevan's peepers, branded bags;
but subject's boots that very dogges disdain'd
are always so-to-speak dead giveaways, my son.

Heeltapper, heeltapper, where have you been?
I've been up my own backside to keep myself clean.
Heeltapper, heeltapper, what did you there?
I passed by a little fact with headroom to spare.

Disheartening in the extreme, no virile bod
of any adoptive gender, colour, class or creed
whatever inducement presents itself desires
to do the act of darkness with his pusser's mother.
Which is not just beige cashmere twin-sets, pearls,
the lingo studiously clipped, the set blue rinse
(they are full-fed with fresh grass from the waist),
but (sob) the end of Classicism as we have known it.
And in that general collapse, high-flying sixth-

former, scent the genesis of incest. Prick an ear!

Honey-trap, honey-trap, where have you been?
I've been up to London to screw a marine.
Honey-trap, honey-trap, what did you there?
I burned a little fact that now we all share.

Go tell it juggins to the judge. Well said or no,
we will not hear of worthy Pioner, that can'st
worke i'th' ground. No shade on leathern wing,
buster, and he shall batten on the body politic ...
now, in the much-meandered ornament about
the lapidary text, the limned initial Word
of What's-her-face, embowered on the page
we have our rubric, and our guttered beasts ...
it is that basilisk again, come back to haunt.
Excess of cunning damnable, their turning our
redoubled triple agent once again will cause
(the cry resounds still silver in the quad,
that offers, *pace* Hume et al., the promise of
material, efficient, formal and at longing last
but no means least your final-type causation)
tenacious groper Mouldwarp, overly adored
since infancy for there is *nothing* absolutely
nothing (let's be blunt). As simply messing
about in holes now is there Ratty my old Soul-
mate to sequester his beloved self snugged up
his own U-fundamental aura po-face. 'Strewth!

Finger man, finger man, where have you been?
I've been up on the rooftops waiting unseen.
Finger man, finger man, what did you there?
I whistled a little lead fact through thin air.

You will be happy with the news: who munches here
on cow-dung sallets does so from a proper desire
of rousing other men into a perception (so we have
it from the Cousins-germaine) of the infinite.
Now there's relief! What's more, both nuts and bolts
and stinks-and-bangs (trust me friends) concur:
the microdot contains the text that doth contain
a microdot the which contains a text that must
perforce contain a microdot O friends it is facile
to write etc. etc. and yes it is (the very truth
be mustered, sized and formed two-deep, my sahib)
turtles turtles turtles all the way down. This does
obtain, if withered now as William oft had hoped
to Truth, despite the promulgations of the Raj.

Shoemaker, shoemaker, where have you been?
I've been transmogrifying a duke to a dean.
Shoemaker, shoemaker, what did you there?
I altered a little fact with loving care.

She rides sidesaddle and must not be spooked.
Our fesnyng was put in and ravening missed
but one, not bad; a perfect purloined bug
inserted as a deaf-aid in her dexter ear
(a print by Hockney, never well received,
but sent to embassies wherever). Did connect
by taught string to an empty can of worms
in darkest Moscow. And she come in ugly, Love!
He, sloven else, makes that and th'action fine.

Burrower, burrower, where have you been?
I've been in the realms of dark Archive's desmene.
Burrower, burrower, what did you there?
I chevied a little fact out into the glare.

He came of another generation that relied
on Orders, bisque strokes, green baize and book codes.
Once one could rest assured, in one's old school
pyjamas, each agent at his left hand handy had
his dog-earedeyednosedthroated and inscribed
prize-day *Crockford* in yapped vellum, gilt.
Or if to interface with our spread-eagled Cousins
who would durst turn a blind eye on it all
obtain by stealth H. Alger's *Bound to Rise.*
State-of-the-Art and nowadays the random bitch
scribbles on one-time pads her one-time poems.

Scalphunter, scalphunter, where have you been?
I've been abroad to bite cords a-twain.
Scalphunter, scalphunter, what did you there?
I infected a little fact to your disrepair.

Safe? Safe as houses! As a three-doored house,
where he is beat about with bladders on a stick
bow wow bow woe who sometime cringing comes,
sometimes, obeyed in upstart office, bites.
The art of our necessities is passing strange
where there are many mansions to be scrounged,
so enter here, to find straw kindly strewn;
a frypan for the kindred chop; the purling loo;
the curtained window that must not be twitched;
the baubl'd goggle box to kill the mortal time;
the telephone as scrambled as Nunc's yolky yegg
(sad, sad Saint Peteman peters out, still stoned)
for She attends ensilvered in the promised main
of light that skulking notwithstanding comes.

Deskman, deskman, where have you been?
I haven't been anywhere, that's where I've been.

Deskman, deskman, what did you there?
I did nothing to nobody nohow nowhere.

You see, Control broke down, and unrepentant wept.
O Soul flesh out the thing itself, inhuman res!
He/she had once been summoned to remembrance,
that we might prophesy the scattering of guise.
There is no patience liken unto that displayed,
if thus bereft, by our pale Lady Minum at the top
left of your screen, my dear; and loveless swear
it is because (no cause no cause what final price
is fortune's fool full circle) she is on the blink
we say because same cursor is Her eyelid as yet un-
identified officially we say but Ile kneele downe
and aske of Angels recognized as Neither-Nor
and come and take upon's the mystery of things ...

For those readers unfamiliar with the novels of John Le Carré, most
of the tradecraft jargon can be found in *Smiley's Circus: A Guide to
the Secret World of John Le Carré* by David Monaghan (Toronto:
Collins, 1986).

I have used and am grateful for the New Penguin *King Lear* (1988)
edited by G.K. Hunter. But in quotation, I have sometimes followed
what seems to me to be the very sensible practice of H.A. Mason,
who argues in *The Tragic Plane* (Oxford: Clarendon Press, 1985) for:

> ... the appearance in quotations of a largely unedited Folio
> Shakespeare when recalling some of the best-known passages
> rather than any modernized text.... My object was to compel a
> sharper attention by offering words both like and unlike those
> with which readers will long have been familiar ...

PART V

Shadows on the Darkened Grass

Cover Her Face with a Black Bandanna, Ma

Something is cooking anyways. Always is, I guess,
down at the dearest chuck wagon. The chores is done,
so I reckon we'll string her up, real slow, because,
be innocent of the knowledge name your poison son,
she gave the sheriff the clap, the filthy scuzz.

Nothing is certain nowadays. Well it always was,
in your oatburners: the bad hombres got themselves kilt,
the best possible posse cut the varmints off at the pass,
but some of the brightest hands died young and fair. Guilt
was, is now and evermore shall be so, a real pain in the ass.

Everything is changed nowadays. But it always has.
In the last staggered reel. Although back then, we cried,
mine eyes dazzle, when the fallen woman, well she was
a painted infelicitous Jezebel who smoked and drank, died:
took one of ten thousand swinging doors like a man does.

That Solipsism Is the Last Refuge of the Loveless

They rock all day, out on the front veranda.
Can spit and fart and whittle in one go.
Philosophers they're not, nor kings of England.
Just like to sit and watch the crabgrass grow.

Most afternoons, they got a crock of moonshine,
by God they'd talk your head off! Athens, Troy,
Jerusalem, you name it and they've been there.
That's how you get to be a good ol' boy.

Time was, real busy late on Friday evenings;
nailed shut on Sundays with the green blinds drawn,
dust-covers on the counters, looked like corpses.
Back open Monday mornings crack of dawn.

There's less and less call hereabouts for cornbread.
Grape soda pop gets fly-specked on the shelf.
No country for the elderly? Exactly –
I couldn't put it better, friend, myself.

We heard her on the crystal set, cat's whisker
pulled her in: Jack Benny's 'Rose in Bloom' –
Thames, Tigris, Nile, Styx, Mississippi, Liffey,
all riverrun through every living room.

Them Campfire Girls, one evening at the Palace,
they peeked backstage, behind the silver screen
to watch the ushers changing; there weren't nothing
but dustballs and loudspeakers to be seen.

So nowadays, you swims against the current,
you got to be Lord Greystoke, or a dunce:
remember, friend, that deep-hole in the Ganges
you only get to put your foot in once.

The good news bubba is, that we're not talking
chopped liver here, nor war-torn Nazareth.
Pull on your pusser's Jesus boots, good buddy,
and walk upon the water. Save your breath.

Your Basic Scenario:
Don't Leave Home without One!

Your mother undiscovered in the garden;
your undiscovered mother in the glass;
your mother hallowed hugely with another;
your hollowed mother mirrored ... let it pass.

Your father hunting rabbits on the commons;
your father feeding rabbits to the snakes;
your father skinning snakes for baby bunting;
your father with his pants down in the jakes.

Just think, my boy; you might have been a Maiden.
And had to tough it out till Mister Right
invited you to scrub his loo, and launder
his filthy smalls, and bear his weight all night.

Remember, miss, you might have been Young Master.
With primogeniture and loveless, schooled to take
it like a man when Man's estate went under.
Just shut your eyes: it's for the Empire's sake.

Beyond recall it all adds up to nothing.
They say they say, there was a mortal sum –
a Conflagration, son: but nothing happened:
Popeyed, you called and still she didn't come.

There is one vacant solace: the amnesic.
You bore a daughter, daughter. If you bled
forever it is done – the childbed scalding.
Gone. The grief is sigil. She is dead.

The question is a matter disremembered
of life and death. A kind of covenantal quiz.
The answer never 'evermore shall be so',
nor ever 'has been', child. It always is.

'What is our guilt? All are naked, none is safe'

Naturalist at Midsummer

Do dolls have souls? All children talk to their toys,
says Baudelaire, and 'the overriding desire
of most children is to get at and
see the soul of their toys.'

– Idris Parry

Hearing a phoebe call,
like a squeezed
Indiarubber doll,
I am seized
by grief: and at length recall

Cutting with great care
from her stout
midriff the valve where
she cried out
to me, self-bereft there.

What Do Poets Want?

It's the ants' pants, it's the bees' knees,
it's the cats' pyjamas O baby please,
it's a broken light for every heart
on Broadway, pal, it's the apple cart
the mob upset on the road of life,
it's roadkill baby, it's man and wife,
it's the fallback beast in the marriage bed,
it's the last erection, the stoned dead
in a zoot suit with an undone zip
and a limp prick and stiff upper lip,

with a reet pleat, and a rough cuff
on a Sunday ear that smarts enough
for a smart kid till queendom come,
it's a soft touch, it's keeping mum
on the casting couch, it's good old dad
in his see-through slip, it's mum gone bad,
it's mum gone off with a travelling man,
it's the kiss of limbo, it's His flight plan,
it's heavenly hate, it's home sweet hell,
it's blood-in-the-pee and a nasty smell
in the waterworks, it's the cells gone ape,
it's homunculus in a tumour's shape,
it's yesterday's press, it's the latest Word,
it's the samurai Damoclesian sword,
it's the daily bread, it's the butterflies
in the old tum-tum, it's ma making eyes
at you not me, it's our fondest dreams
come false again, it's childbed screams,
it's the screaming kids, it's our Heavenly Pa,
it's the me-me's screaming – about your jaw –
real sorry, baby, that's how things are,
you ought to know that a good cigar
is a good cigar, but a naughty wench
is only another well-ploughed trench,
you ought to know, to go up in smoke
and mirrors, mate, is a smutty joke,
it's the ark careened, it's a livelong zoo,
it's the whole boiling, the least tabu,
it's all dark promise, what's come to pass,
it's jet death in the blazed glass,
it's the living end, it's the mortal taint,
– but, Siggy, baby, – you it ain't.

———

Two Poems of Some Complexity

Progenitors

It was a message, and inscribed on stone,
that only their priest-caste could understand;
or so they told us and they *must* have known.

To be a Daniel and to stand alone,
with hogsheads of testosterone to hand:
it was a message and inscribed on stone,

not mortal clay. The blade cut to the bone
but missed the physic nodule of the gland;
or so they told us. And they must have known

that while we waited by the telephone
all bloody day the switchboard was unmanned!
It was a message and, inscribed on stone,

beyond dispute that God would not condone
this sacrilege. In fact it went as planned.
Or so they told us – and they must have known,

they left it there, half buried in the sand,
defaced of course, on coming to this land.
It was a message. And inscribed on stone.
Or so they told us. And they must have known.

Of Love's Complaint

From this the poem springs: that we live in a place
That is not our own and, much more, not ourselves
And hard it is in spite of blazoned days.
                                        – Wallace Stevens

Which one's our own?
I told you that I waited by the telephone
all bloody day ... ah, dear heart, you know ...
well, never mind. And much, much more: although
I really hoped and prayed, prostrate, like anything,
it didn't ring.

Which one's ourself?
I prowled, dear heart, shelf after endless shelf
and cracked each book and stormed each fly-specked page,
and found some order in the sacred rage:
but what muezzin from minaret sang out, 'Is land ahoy?'
No bloody joy.

Which blazoned days?
What constant sacrament (*ars longa*, mate) of praise?
I have of blue Susanna sung elsewhere.
And even seen her standing dear heart bare
in her cheval-glass yes in that bright-blazed regard.
It's bloody hard.

Whose poem springs?
An old dog blooded sings, and louder sings:
of *vita brevis*, mate. Both yours and mine.
But to have swanned across the starting line
as one, sweet heart, about our native radiant place,
is no disgrace.

——

Of Woman's Last Obedience

A Quick Tumble in Eden

A thing as lovely as a tree – San Francisco *Chronicle*

To bring the forest primeval inside, USG interiors, the well-known manufacturers of acoustic tile, has created Interior Trees, 19-foot-tall artificial trees made of aluminum and steel.

USG's Merritt Seymour told Metropolis magazine that the company's design team had been looking for a product that would be a metaphor for a better life. Trees, which provide shelter and help purify the air, fit the bill. 'We wanted to create a product that could contribute positively to a person's well-being, whether it's used in a health-care setting, a restaurant, a mall or an office,' Seymour said.

Interior Trees look like a cross between a sun umbrella and a tree. Trunks have electrical outlets, phone hookups and vents for air circulation. The lowest 'branches' have lamps; above that are 'large palm-like fronds' of microperforated steel, says Metropolis, 'which seem to shift slightly – as the eye travels across them.'

The designers visualize the trees standing in large rooms and functioning as spatial anchors. Groups of desks can be clustered around them.

(from the Toronto *Globe and Mail*, 18 September 1996.)

When Adam delved and Eve span
God was then a gentleman:

When Eve scrumped while Adam delved
The plan of Paradise was shelved.

When Eve smirked while Adam scrumped –
Then the two-backed beast was humped!

When Eve and Adam were sent spinning
God foresaw no end of sinning:

When Adam delved Eve to the bone
God came. Into His own.

Quinquireme of Nineveh

... an immense world of delight, clos'd by your senses five ...
                                        – William Blake

Sorry, matey, that's my tin ear.
It gets harder and harder to tell
Judith from Judas; a moment ago
I could have sworn Philomel
was sifting away in the convent – say,
has the sexton toll'd the bell?

And what if the universe stinks worse
that anyone *can* suppose?
Christ! is that a noisome fart?
A herring? A red red rose?
Chanel number 666? Incense,
or brimstone burnt? God knows.

We're out of touch with our feelings, love.
The tangible's not the same
as it was when we had at our fingertips,
just a moment ago, your Name;
well it's hard to say if one's not wearing
one's shirt of hair or of flame.

It's junk food: cheese or chalkburgers.
So go water your single malt
whisky, Miranda, to your taste:
they swear that the savour of salt
(it was yours we have eaten) nowadays
is lost. Well, it's not *their* fault.

But the eyes are okay and have it still.
You were asking about the light?
It was going faster and faster, dear,
when last seen late last night,
going like Hell in a handbasket,
right out of Immortal sight.

The Price of Admission

The Impoverished Scientist wept buckets
into his frayed turn-ups as he discovered
in quicksilver spilled the long-lost short
formula for the Alkahest: a one-reeler
with a beginning and a middle and an end.

Past master of slapstick, he cracked up
to see his act reassembled, seamless
(the film had been run for him backwards)
but sans yolk, and had to be shipped off
in restraining harness to the funny farm.

During a power breakfast, the swarthy King
of Spaghetti Westerns signed One Meatball
as top gun, gaffer and best boy. Not a bad
morning's work, for a green kid who come up
from Next-to-Nothing, somewhere in Brooklyn.

Scenting manumission, the Cast of Thousands
bent, tore, folded, spindled and otherwise
mutilated their computer-cards and flowed
as one woman, like joyous lemmings, over
the precipice into Esther Williams' pool.

When Oliver (or was it Stan?) had shinnied
up to the top of the Pasadena lamp-post
and lit a match, he could read the sign:
'Wet Paint'. God being reputedly moribund,
he favoured us with his best slow burn.

Monarch of all he surveys at the Office,
Daddy admonished his wayward daughter
(she had already slept with the nebbish)
to no avail; he would have, it would seem,
to sign, with his Parker 99, the Big Cheque.

Well I will tell you, lootenant, where all
them bleep Injuns come from: Cultural Casting.
And the hosses from Knacker's Rent-A-Cayuse,
likewise. The question is, podner, after
the last Massacre where are they all going?

Packard don't make them like that any more; black;
with running boards that could carry two G-men
each, their tommy-guns blazing; with headlights
like half a nacelle; with windshields that open.
There are, ephebe, no getaways left for the Mob.

Informal Portrait

He didn't cash in on the sweeps,
marry a title, scale Mt. Garbage,
or square the circle; he can't
juggle, almost drowned in the loo.

Has been punched out by bikers,
denounced from the pulpit, won't
finish his novel, doesn't floss,
smokes after intercourse, votes.

And if he were deaf, he'd sport
an ear-trumpet huge as a tuba,
of silver, with gold scrollwork,
and demand that you bellow down it.

Or, were he stricken spud-blind,
he'd be led to expensive fleshpots
by a seeing-eye belly dancer
in diaphanous lime pantaloons.

Crippled, he'd scatter accountants
in a souped-up Ferrari bath chair
with a Hollywood muffler and chrome
horns that go 'Phart! Phart!'

He has, in fact, most of his God-
given faculties (he can't smell;
but he doesn't regret it) and
it is difficult not to like him.

Service

Guess what (no prizes)? No; not that there is no Nobodaddy,
honing Old Testament dirty tricks to perfection in solitude,
lurking behind or within the massive tumid organ which
in skilled hands can almost bring one to believe in Bach:
but He never was, was He? Well, we knew this all along,
of course; but it passed, oft-times, for a necessary fiction.

And, that the stark light that floods through the blood-
stained glass to splatter the ogive with colour beyond
the wildest dreams (so we are told: how do they *know?*)
of lap-dogs, falls, to employ an archaic verb, from the only
sun, our very own day star, to which we are all hopelessly
indentured, is common knowledge. They teach it in school.

And it's not that at six o'clock no Mummy and Daddy
will take you home again because you're tired little
of being bullied by big girls who can get you down
with a knee on your chest and give you a knuckle head-
rub and a wrist burn and, when at last you cry, jeer 'Sissy!'
or 'Cowardy custard!' Because when they both died
you knew it. It was explicit. Like sex. Just as natural.

And it's not *(sweet Jesus!)* even the evident fact at three
a.m. that there but for the Goddess of Grace it could be you
in the cage framed small to ensure that you can't turn, kept
in your own squitter and total darkness and fed slop, weak
as a veal calf (that can't mind): a house-guest of Pol Pot.

No, as a matter of fact, it's good news. The answer, I mean.
Well, it's only that, even if with much ado we were corrupted,
and made to learn the dirty devices of this world, somebody
loves us all. No, not the Esso folk who for profit kowtow
to an over-all black translucency, to darkness visible. No,
it's somebody like (there was nobody like) Elizabeth Bishop.
And that, if on a good day we are all weighed and found wanting,
she still loves somehow undeserving us. So, what else is new?

Cruise

Three wise men of Gotham
Went to sea in a bowl.
If the bowl had been stronger,
My story would have been longer.

And if we do make landfall at long last, well, I ask you: what then?
What if that verdigris-blue-green node on the brazen horizon-line
(the which we admire each morning and by sanguine sunset loathe)
is transmogrified into Royal Guano Island, notorious in travelogues
for the ferocity of its scabrous rats, its infestations of sallow leeches,
its lingering stinks, the relentless avarice of its sullen indigenes?

What do you crave, friend, in your vagabond heart: reality or rumour?
Love (if you'll pardon the word), or the clippity-clap and penicillin?
If you have residual doubts, consult the steward, a Calvinist. In fact,
like most islands hereabouts it's the tip of a once-fulminating volcano,
long dormant in our dead reckoning of things. Which is what matters.

Listen, it wasn't for any miasmatic backwater roadstead I found the ready.
Read your brochure: if it's glitz, it's still a contract, I'll hold them to it,
they'll hear from my lawyers if the carcinogenic sun doesn't abound down
all the livelong-happy-hour day and Circe's courtesy drinks aren't triples!
But I'll tell you something for heartbreaking nothing, my shipboard mate:
when you've seen one honest-to-God miracle, you've seen the bloody lot.

Actually, the two of you have met – *she* remembers – but it's been ages;
oh, she's skulking below decks, having her hair done before the meridian,
just in case she should decide, if we ever get there, to go ashore after all.

Admonition, *Ipse Dixit,* from Afar

I met the nonce-word-maddened Muse of Torquemada
(the lamented cruciverbalist, not the rigorist Spaniard),
    tireless for Goddess's greater glory. She declaimed:

'Detachment may grant a human perspective, a chance
    transformation: this must not be learnèd. A walking
    on clear water over the scudded reflection of heavens
    above and below savants, the which are star-crossed.

'As propinquity scatters loose clues. As perilous scree,
    heaped piecemeal under the cloud of unknowing-
    swirled, vertical peak: the surmised shards of self-
inflicted misprision; of closet meanders; of guesswork.

'Love, summoned, casts myriad hints. Of the bittersweet
fragrance of lapse, perhaps. Perhaps of the darling Joker,
    still pissing herself laughing – as yet *aiaiai* to come to
    pass. And beware,' she added, squinting into the dark,

'of the first person singular.'

Eschatological Thoughts

It was never a question that could
be entirely resolved, made exact
in the fleet Jesuitical mind
of the Father: whether for better
or worse, past conceivable doubt,
there were mosquitoes in Eden;

but one thing he knew for certain:
in the swampy *Anopheles* south
it may well be a different matter,
but if you had managed to land
on North Garden Island, the black
flies would have driven you mad.

> *Whenever the elastic that's*
> *death's*
> *slapstick snaps back whap!*

Rabbi, remember the long night
when God was a Past Master;
we were *warranted* a terrific show,
if the dress was a disaster!

Listen, maybe we weren't that fast,
and maybe not all that clever –
but in the beginning nobody said
that nothing goes on forever.

So look at the players left unscathed –
here's where it gets real scary:
that hopeless nebbish, that fall guy, Tom
and his plaguey trickster, Jerry.

Adversary

Sweetheart, I'm sorry, always being the fall guy,
  having to break it to you. But never presume:
  it's not Her lughole that's glued to the tumbler
  against the liver-spotted wall in the next room.

She wouldn't let Herself be caught half-living
  in a tenth-rate, rented dump like this. No way.
  Omnipotent or not, Milady could never stomach
  those beige drapes with the violet floral spray,

or the crusted midden of last night's dirty dishes
  shoved under an enseamèd bed. She'd have a fit
  at the ashtrays, reeking with crook cigar butts:
  after all those aeons, cold turkey, She just quit.

Perhaps it's your mother-in-law, eavesdropping,
  or your first husband; hey, whatever you prefer,
  for a furtive, delicious pang of vicarious guilt:
  how in sweet Hell would I know? But it's not Her.

Don't forget, She's been there, forever and ever;
  done that, dark everywhere. As matter of fact,
  She's more or less at liberty these days; besides,
  She likes things nice, after being a first-class act.

Anyway it's all changed, with the new liturgy.
  She doesn't give a toss any more, as you know,
  if another broken, embarrassing body suffers,
  dying and rising again: well, quid pro quo.

Lines for the
Dominion Observatory
Time Signal

I hate to have to tell you this,
it offends the proprieties, for
you are a guest in our house;
and in time we have welcomed
within these four walls Erato
and Baby Snooks and Polyhymnia,
and Amos and Andy and Clio
and even the disembodied voice
of William Lyon Mackenzie King's
mamma in petulant reprimand
(quantula sapientia regatur mundus).

Sir, or madam, know our abode
is chockablock with clocks,
all ticking away awaiting
exactitude. We all after all
long for the one sure Truth;
and our dial, which can span
Alpha and back from Omega
with one quick flick is ready-
set to receive your steadfast
assignation, the blinds drawn,
the baked meats in the fridge,
the note composed and the heart-
beat as steady as death; yet,
dear friend, the fact remains

that even after the longest dark
dash unknown to man the time
will still prove suspect. But
keep looking. For we have pinned
such faith on your heavenwards-
yearned, great glass eye. O

keep looking. Keep keep keep
keep keep keep keep keep keep …

PART VI

A Pace of Change

Elsewhere

A beginning and a muddle and an end. Clever.
'No young man believes that he will ever die.'
It is Thursday again; the garbage goes out.

And Bede's sparrows have carried strands of grass
into the top branches of the fitful beech,
they stream in the aimless formulaic wind.

'The lie is the specific evil which man
has introduced into nature.' We live
and we die by our fictions nevertheless.

So you turn to me and with a chance remark
kindle the landscape it is become diamond-
burning eternal an instant. Thus

Bardolph is well hung and Mistress Quickly
is riggish and poor Hal goes forth to lead
wolves to their slaughter of God even

while one Man babbled of green fields
in Eastcheap. We stand or fall, desire
winnowed in showers of countless arrows.

Full Circle

The mast a radius, given
the steep triangular sail
with diagonal parallel seams,
the converged vectors of rigging.

But when the sail, a translucent lime
bordered with sanguine, bellies
in the importunate captious wind,
the seams are seen as sweet arcs;

And ropes, alack and alas, slacken
and tauten as winds veer, strengthen,
diminish, die over altered water.
The hull is a constant flourish, granted;

But when, late last night, you said
that the light is rebuffed,
you were right, as always,
of course, and wrong.

Remark

The shaft of sunlight strikes
aslant Aunt Agatha's headstone,
and nothing happens. No matter.

Nor do we excavate barrows
or tumuli, hoping to meet up with
good old Uncle Joe. Oh no.

Our progenitors were not Giants.
Our progeny are not homunculi.
The war was the Great War, of course.

But when you turn, and mention
that one side of the perched crow
is a slab of momentary silver

and the other a jet blot in the light-
soaked oak, we may entertain
again transitory, insufficient, death.

Around and About

(in memory of P.S.)

What we forget, my dear, in our good fortune,
Is that everything is what we almost had.
We are impressed by seasons and rich uncles,
As well indeed we should be, and are glad.

The heat-death of the living sun is abstract.
The sun, by day, is real and iron clad.
And yet we look askance, or are embarrassed,
Or gaze on moons instead, which is too bad.

I knew a house in London, but it crumbled.
Because of death and taxes. Well, sad, sad.
Boiled shirts; hair shirts; stuffed shirts; and mostly dirty.
Sir Harold was a bounder, Bert a cad.

Eliot thought we probably had missed it.
Auden knew a fashion from a fad.
Yeats was still a virgin in his thirties.
Rilke watched the captive panther pad.

The trouble is that some remember mother
And swear that they remember good old dad.
The sun was once a tempest in a teacup.
The actual is abstract. Men go mad.

Aftermath of a Conversation

Red blood from the red gills of lumpen fishes
dries on the parched dock. And this is true:
one can imagine having anything one wishes.
Most men don't torture children. But some do.

Admittedly, one can imagine even being wise
in the intolerable ways of man, should he so dare.
The gull, you said, settled to pick out the living eyes
of stranded salmon; my dear, you do not care

to answer anyone in kind, and not from pride.
To be inhuman sometime fits us like God's glove.
Who may imagine us as creatures who deride
their being God, and being very terrible to love.

Against the First Idea

From what was then Ceylon, this elephant –
elegant, porcelain, abstract – came crammed
with tea like brittle, sage-green iron filings.

Lustrous, the smoke-white glaze absorbs
the ambient refracted light. Caparison
is worked with sanguine-umber foliage
unfurled, and cursive patterns repeat
elaboration on draped back and flanks;
the forehead bears a various-phased moon,
an ament-likeness sun; two beehive-
headed deities are figured, fore and aft.

Six toes detailed in dull gold; one
gold rose adorns each temple; gold
caps on stumped tusks; feathered gold
on trapping-fringes. Resplendent, as becomes
brash Ganesh on garish Holy Days.

The natural elephant discovered in the so-
called wild is also elegant, ears flared,
unravelling deep jungle's emerald loft;
trunk cunning, stretching delicate for some
gloom-ripened succulence: but not abstract.

Nor is the so-called natural elephant,
when held in man's captivity, abstract.
No. Instructive, certainly: it will not do,
is untoward, perhaps, to dwell on this.

Most things may be, indeed on feast days all
things are, instructive; and often elegant as well.
Which, mind, is not to say that elephants imagined
in surreal drawing-rooms are not abstract. They are,
but not in mortal terms, which are the most
that most of us, unlike immortal elephants
trumpeting across the glitter-goes of tanks,
of man-made waterways, will ever bear.

Reticulations

In profile out of Euclid when erect, they are
a standing carnal theorem. And to drink
become corollary, a most amazing folding down
between their rigid canted forelimbs. Truth!

And they are wading shoulder-shallow through
their dense partaking medium, the air,
bearing above their sea-horse-bended necks
their sea-horse heads. When born, they fall
six feet to mother earth, the keeper said:
rude wakening. Their wetblack vastlashed eyes
discarded us, beyond the pale, as scholar's jaws
took up their interrupted chomp once more.

And did I mention that their tongues sometimes
flick viperquick, or sometimes stick like chub
of blueblack gutta-percha from their mouths,
or briefly probe a nostril? I think not.

Or that each bears, beyond the merely logical
completion of a bony tail, a tassel-whisk
resembling much those shrunken trophy heads,
with long black coarsened hair, from Borneo?

It is an old temptation, is it not, to look
upon their like and mutter, 'QED'?

Watchers

Dun shadows from shadow embodied, the several deer,
five whitetail does, drift out of the woods at dusk.

Hesitant, wary, feral survivors, they pick their way
over the whorled snow as if across tufts of embers,

freezing in half-stride for long moments, become
sculpture, their heads lifted to scent presence,

to hear in the charged silence the least heartbeat.
And abrupt, with a casual tail-flick, continue

towards the desired corn we have scattered under
the stripped white ash. Where at last they browse,

their forelegs carefully splayed, their shagged necks
lowered like freighted branches, briefly, then snatched

upright in sudden caution, muzzles raised, their ears
constantly swivelled. They assume in the moonlight

themselves and their cast shadows a single intricate
creature, the eye is confounded, they pass through

each other's prolonged bodies, their too-delicate legs
commingle, they are one woven molten night-animal

beheld grazing on furtive darkness. At our slightest
gesture they vanish. Some of them are gravid.

Three Acts of Homage

Doggerel
(for I. W.)

While consciousness defines
what consciousness postpones,
say this of disrepair:
we may not make old bones.

But let us entertain
this reason to rejoice:
at every doomed advance
we are embroiled in choice

within this seeming farce
of promise or of curse,
of battleground or truce,
fool's Paradise, or worse,

prop carrot and real stick.
It still remains to prove
your evident, vouchsafed
and huge consensus, Love.

Sequel, Sans Parting
(for J.C.R.)

There were ghosts, of unctuous enemies and arch lovers,
of disingenuous friends, that had to be laid to rest;
but at last she finished her fulsome confessional letter.
She had done, she could tell herself, her dishonest best.

It was couched in code. But one that might be deciphered.
Ergo: given voracious intelligence, it would be read.
It was not written on impulse, or from studied desperation.
Nor did milady repent her of anything she had said.

She did not touch on the inconstancies of weather;
nor on her well-being, hale at the worst of times;
nor did she dwell on her decorous chinless husband,
or his snivelling brats. And not on her own sweet crimes.

She burned the false starts, the crumple of fool-papers,
making one fair copy in an elegant chancery-hand.
She was fully aware of the weakness inherent in argument
by analogy. But he of all mortal creatures would understand.

If he did not ... but that was vastation beyond her compass.
She had entertained terror often, and sometimes fear.
The salutation demanded of her a most delicate malice;
she settled on lethal insinuation: 'O my dear ...'

Only when it was signed, with an alias, and enveloped
in blanched vellum cut from unblemished skins,
the spluttered crimson impressed with his own sigil,
and despatched post-haste, did she reconsider her sins.

And found them wanting! This was the fearful gravamen
that she levelled against herself. And she railed at fate
for the fistful of laws she unwittingly had left unbroken:
and sent to retrieve her letter. Of course too late.

Collide, Collide
(for R. F.)

The whirligig, Gyrinidæ,
has split its compound eyes. To see
and fathom one reality,

half is suspended, that this dread
pond-water predator be fed,
beneath the margin of the head,

where it can constantly survey
prospective palatable prey
in underwater disarray.

The upper portion of each pair
is so positioned, it can stare
throughout the diamond midday air

above the waters' face, to learn
of predators that would discern
and feed upon it in their turn.

And may in frenzied circles find
reprieve: or replicate, defined
by like gyration of its kind.

Too soon to thank our lucky stars
we don't go wild like dodgem cars
about our lusts and loves and wars:

blind providence may yet divide
our single vision. Or provide
us none at all. Collide, collide!

Virus

Beyond the vicious surf, the scrub foreshore,
bruised foothills are aligned,
then realigned:

and sailors swear assuredly thereby
that mountains are removed.
This northern coast

seems uninhabited. No flickered lights
by night, no sudden tufts
of smoke by day,

to disconcert the heart returned, aghast,
from broken promises –
those shimmered sands,

those ripened islands smouldering. That fade
like shame below the seared
horizon line.

Like recollection. Inland here, they say,
replenishing the soul
sweet rivers rise ...

Immortal

But you do not die because you are sick,
you die because you are alive.

– Montaigne

You who assume
in our bright blinding all
forever-tendered, ever-
mortal guise,

in whomsoever's
outraged gaze endures
the laced flame-adders'
always eyes ...

You who resume
to our spun day star some
late, rare, bewildered
god's surmise,

where self consumed,
our shrunken sun become
most massy fireclove,
kindles, dies ...

Sideglance

i *Elder at Daybreak*

Here is a whet of knife.
Here is a shim of light.
Here am I, terrified
before this bloody sun that died –
riven out of night,
risen into life.

ii *Social Graces*

Found, blowing in the gutter:
it was Death's bread-and-butter
letter.

He, while disinclined
to answer it in kind,
had better.

III *Death's-head*

Above our vicious circle turns
the poxed and farded moon,
in ignorant night.

We prize her constancy, have held
her comely and, just once,
have touched her face,

unlovingly. She heaves our seas –
the seasons of ourselves.
Ah, love, let us

be false in her deflection lest
we fail, in this flamed world,
to incandesce.

IV *Beholder*

Look! Into the shuddered sun
up from the jaundiced dust
the lithe stripling shinnies O
he shinnies up and vanishes
into the bare firmament O no
mirrors O no ropes of smoke.

When on love intent. Then

the venomed cobra swayed
erect in flickered dissonance
in shrill insistence weaving
woven in the nagging raga
drops through thundered silence
into its captive basket back.

The lid is gingerly replaced.

v *Eclipse*

Over and over and over it takes
we are told an iron will
in this iron night to bind us.

There is no lost light forsakes
the archaic Chalice – no silver spill
seeps silver desirous to find us.

No. Gold day, it is spoken, breaks.
Love, we are less than love until
death comes, to remind us.

vi *Hinterland*

Where rivers are unsilted,
a long way from the coast,
in the Virgin's garden
dwells the Holy Ghost.

I guess. It is not given
to us, instinct with dream
from childhood, and rapacious,
to swim upstream.

———

VII *Only over Another Horizon*

It is chill amber, autumn, the days
  diminish, with water afire
    in the distant mirror:

    where I watch you

  ah, turning, and walking away
    toward the immortal silver,
      no one is nearer.

VIII *Error in Mirror in Error*

Then let him glance sideways,
Abandon a balance,
A sometimes precarious burden,

The lever and great beam in its span,
In its single appointed sweep
Over the massive pivot

And excellent burnished wheel,
The no longer incredible circle
Denied, an impaired turning

And all, all for a frailty, a flaw
In a brilliant foible, a maybe
Divine improper or other Human figure.

Jonah as Boy Seaman

Acknowledgement of Orders.

The seaman acknowledges an order with the words 'Aye Aye, Sir!'
and should then immediately carry it out.

(*Manual of Seamanship*, vol. I B.R. 67 [I/51]
London: His Majesty's Stationery Office, 1951, p. 265)

He longed to cram it all into his purser's chest
and chuck it overboard, the whole entangled botch;
and tell his captain he was making a clean breast
of things, and volunteer to stand the middle watch.

Or else evade his mother's eye, her weary shrug,
while she was in the kitchen making him his tea,
and sweep the broken vow beneath the threadbare rug
that stretched across the room from sea to sea.

Fear, whatever depths that filial guilt may plumb,
can rise and drift ashore upon some filthy tide;
and he foresaw stout men in blazoned aprons come
to take the carpets up when she had barely died.

And there is no away to get to, or to throw
the neighbours' garbage into; nor could he let
his vade mecum perish, with its crazy row
of patchwork numbers and its dog-eared alphabet.

Disrepair

In *The Book of Rules and Repudiation* it is written:
that Moira eloped, ran off with Count What's-his-face,
that doddering, impotent, affluent nonagenarian!
They had, the paparazzi, a field day with this disgrace.

It is small consolation, to know that bluebirds are nesting
for the third year in a row in Cynthia's cedar box.
Ben has abandoned his high hopes that the purple martins
will solve the mosquito problem. But money talks.

Meanwhile it appears, in the Middle East and elsewhere,
right here at home, for example, that things just might,
any second now, go critical in the Religious reactor.
It is something to take to heart. Well, Swift was right.

We can always fall back, of course, on Hoyle and Roberts.
More fallen women, they know the rules (and carry mace
on Main Street at midday) of men's games and conventions,
than ever before concur: 'The Soul is its own place.'

Neither-Nor

There are intrigues, Byzantine intricacies afoot, Zendik;
much scurrying through the Blue Mosque, around and about Hagia
Sophia. Some euphemists call it 'Queen of the Sciences'.

Others, gobbledegook. For having broken open the golden egg,
there are always geese who would have it repaired soonest.
The which, thin schoolmen remonstrate, is easier done than said.

Meanwhile, back at the Vatican, learned fathers consider
the Lobachevskyan geometry, not of Canaveral's minarets,
but of Master Piero della Francesca's transfixed Madonnas.

Parallel lines do meet, of course, and greet one another,
if hyperbolically, exchange salutations in their becoming
courtesy and diverge on the several errands of several God

be praised! Allah be praised! O Maiden, had you put on,
darkening, disentangled, before the indifferent Angel
could let you fall flat His power with His knowledge ...

Speaking of Money

The narrative rambles through tilled, familiar country
in a circumlocutional manner, as narratives often do.
The elders were highly respected for long digressions.

The bailing tin with a decalcomania of Prince Albert
puffing his calumet rusts in the dugout bottom,
sloshing in rainbows and roses of spilled petrol.

The women have long forgotten which slippery inner barks
and fetid roots and berries and pungent leaves
might be chewed as a vermifuge. But it doesn't matter.

In the kinship myths, it was only your mother's uncles'
female cousins' daughters … but it's Sunday, the menfolk
are all stoned, sprawled in their bark-rope hammocks.

We will come to the point; at least, if we don't miss it;
which may prove to be an unexploded locofoco cigar.
Where there's fire there's smut and no impractical jokes.

What the Man in Undress Said

Putting aside kid gloves, top hat,
his caracul-collared greatcoat that
secretes a vermilion lining, stripped
of borrowed gongs, his boiled shirt ripped
away in a fusillade of studs,
divested of all of his formal duds,
shedding in one convulsive flux
his Griswold Lorillard heritage tux,
his patent leather pumps, silk socks
and delicate lavender smalls, he stalks
birthday-suited towards the door –
the one that he entered once before.

And utters his shibboleth: 'Forsooth!'
This being his boast, his naked truth,
doubtless. Yeats, damn his eyes,
collared the market with 'enterprise'.

A Life in the Day of Mr Joy

And hereof had they as great marvel, that some of them
trowed it were an impossible thing to be.

– Mandevilles's Travels

Landfall, with palms like houris' lashes
along the horizon! And the confident
quicksilver river running uphill!
What consummate marvels! Lonely men
have died for more. Meanwhile, beholden,
I must harrow the quotidian: and contrive
another chapter in the brash narrative of
Captain Balderdash, adventurer, who twice
betook himself to darkest foreign parts.

To death: and back again. Together with
the tempered instruments that unplucked gave
grave strain, to which attendant beasts
of reason harkened and were strangely tamed.

We will survive our fictions, it is said.
And so I could believe, had I not heard
it first, myself, as pillow-talk from her
who held me once thus incandescent with
the cinder'd Phoenix risen from her flame.

A Particular Tree on the Lawn

Let it be said of this comely, purple-leaved plum:
it provides perch for the intricate-plumed birds
that evade thereby even bright-whetted words
of noontide adumbration, of what may come.

Say that it survives its swarming green surround;
that its flourishing brings a various light to mind,
one we would not be enabled otherwise to find,
save for this purple burnished above groomed ground.

And remark black shadow cast, where the sward is mown;
Its roots are blind-life-in-darkness-white at the core.
The which we have both encountered heretofore.
I would elaborate, love, but the phrase is flown.

A Stain on the Page

If here, before our very eyes, one jot
or tittle, one minuscule mote should move
and, probably impossible thereby,
in this minute particular disprove

the given human burden of discourse,
this least volition of one worldly grain
would cast us back upon haphazard seas,
adrift on chartered darkness once again.

Yet should this sole subversive speck display,
if magnified, six rudimentary legs
and slubbed antennae, know that nowadays
our scrupulous attention only begs

the beggared question: neither haggard god
is entertained, Magister, to propose;
nor bestial man, inanimate or not,
in greater apprehension to dispose.

As one who crushes wayward insects knows.

Her Account of Calenture

Having crossed the equator,
there I was up in the stone-
the-crows-nest, knocking back
Dr Bee's tar-water extract
against the vapours, the heaves,
staggers and female complaint,
when the dimmed binnacle slow-
see-sawing fathoms below
my motley-hung crosstrees
went suddenly ape and by God
there *he* was, large as life,
walking, babbling, across
the emerald-furrowed fields,
having a hissy-fit, slashing
the heads off starwort, lady-
smock, nightshade and thistle,
selfset at impossible odds
on a crooked collision course
with our bottom-fouled bum-
boat! Lordy, what a to-do!

The bosun had barely dressed
all hands mustered amidships,
with killicks set ramrod
ready to pipe him aboard,
when with only a die's throw
to go a voracious great
pink shark slashed
up through the greensward

sending incarnadine divots
flying to Volans and snatched
him unbelievable! under,
leaving a crimson foot-
print swirled, moiled,
upon the smaragdine turf.

And thus was the ship's
manifest company saved
to the last soul in the nick
of what passes for time.

PART VII

The Flight out of Egypt

Millefleur

I

Which goes without saying. Of course. So I will say it.
Even though it will still go. On its own sweet way;
there not being another modus vivendi ready to hand.

So the cat is let out of the undiplomatic bag at last;
Kilkenny cats are cut down from the taught line. O
that this too too fluid world were Euclidean, which it's not.

For the shortest long-distance call between two points
is a vast abysm. Dark backwards, perhaps; who knows?
Ah, not the poor disembowelled mogs. To see such sport ...

we are left with the proof negative; the bloodied tales
offered as evidence of things best left unseen. You learn
early on to wipe that silly grin from your face in class.

What's-his-name swings at a change-up, lo and away,
and it's going, going, gone into the fair firmament!
The crowd goes wild, and this year's pennant is cinched.

Or at half-mast. Because somebody loses, regrettably,
whenever the brave wins. And the halyards get tangled
together wherever an ill wind blows, for better or worst.

But every body is safe at first. And we quickly learn
in this vale of soul-making to steal second. Because,
if the porch light is on, the whole team is out at home.

'I calls them as I sees them.' Doughty; and fair enough.
'I calls them as they is.' But what of the Enlightenment?
'Until I calls them, they ain't.' Ah. Well. That's it then.

And he had dreamt, who hasn't, of spending his last days
perched at the end of the jetty, mending his obsolete nets,
watching the buckled light burn in the ebb and flow.

Just watching the boats returning, burdened with life,
sunk to the gunwales with silver, manned by the young
with tired backs turned to the saffron-and-rose horizon.

Who, content with the sea's provision, the day's abundance,
might glance landward and, just out of earshot, smile
at the sight of the old seadog ensconced on a rusted bollard.

Who sings to himself of the death of Swift. Of Johnson mad
with agony, attempting to lance his own leg. Of the lives
and the deaths of poets. Of Johnson composing his *Prayers*.

IV

In the disavowed dark. It would appear, we have all darkest
Africa and her prodigies in us. And as well, for darkness'
measure, that 'motive without a mind', the emergent virus.

Yet darkness attends us; if there be not impossibilities
enough in Religion for an active faith, remember there is
the possible to reconsider. They have all gone into the dark.

And speaking of light, as we always are when darkness
looms in the alcoves of dangerous rooms, in stairwells where
we descend blindly together, it might be weighed in the mind.

And found wanting. Sadly in fact, to be transported is not
to be transfigured. Most of us will have, now and again,
suffered the little redemptive death. Few of us are saints.

V

She blows smoke rings on the sea shore. Where there's fire ...
And what's a torus more or less in the teeth of the ragèd gale?
She'll stay no more on the burning shore so let the music play.

She sang beyond the genius of the sea: what did she sing?
How smoke blinded her eyes; how her quondam pals deride,
laughing, the kindled pillow-talk of Dr Jekyll and Mr Hyde.

'Okay, Beldame, where's the fire?' 'In the slow lane, Officer-
of-the-Law.' Between the advancing combers phosphor flames
shudder the endless furrows, aligned from the setting sun.

The waves were fired. Meanwhile the black smoke rose,
spiralled over the ghats where we weep gharial tears.
It was the sea, not she, that the last light incandesced.

VI

Well last things first. Our motto for today or yesteryear.
So we still stand dumbfounded in the knot-quite-Garden
naming things out of sight. Not, mind you, out of mind.

From which we cannot be delivered. Nor alas consoled.
Because the body beautiful in youth and garlanded goes tick,
goes tock. It is the oldest wheeze and when we laugh it hurts!

There is no end to telling it anew: where brightness falls,
if scattered helter-skelter with the wind like ripened seed,
there is enough of incorruption in a glance, a glancing blow.

We do not cling for dear death like the drowning man to chaff
who have been, will be shrived in silver rain, eclipsed in light
unlaced amain, the casual touch in passing of beloved hands.

'... after the waterbrooks'

Beneath the summer's palsied sun I bend
to drink. The nearby wading pool is clean,
just filled and faintly acrid with chlorine.
A toddler squatting in the shallow end

slaps at the kindled water, tries to stand,
collapses briefly, squats again and squeals
mock terror. Her pregnant mother wheels
a stroller through a ragged spill of sand,

then, awkward, spreads a blanket in the bright
shadow of a spruce. Her brother lugs
a crimson plastic pail; she hunkers, hugs
herself and wallows, screaming her delight.

And suddenly love sears upon my mind
that image of a naked napalmed child,
much publicized – a foreign girl defiled
by foreign fire: and flame enraged to blind

the sun in unfamiliar flesh unfurled
is burning unconsumed, and in the same
Conflagration I straighten to proclaim
that nothing is negated in this world.

Souls on a Bus Station Bench

'for the joy of love is too short, and the sorrow thereof,
and what cometh thereof, dureth over long.'

Malory, *Le Morte D'Arthur*, x. lvi

What, sixteen? Huddled, asleep and crumpled together,
both heavily into the chrome hardware and scuffed black leather;

he with a single pinchbeck earring, she with one nostril pearl,
her kohl smeared, her lashes tacky, her plumpknuckled, little-girl

hand with the quickbitten nails curled into his gangrel's fist,
huge, crude-skull-tattooed, lump-stuck on the end of his wrist;

neither overly clean, nor, like most of us, probably overly sane;
heads fledgling-shaved, save for a Mohawk, a formal roached mane;

his a rare, Edwardian, delicate violet, hers a lime Popsicle green
Christ! grant us compassion admonished compassion we have all been

there, sullen, too close to the incandesced bone, mute, ferret-feral
entangled *O noli me tangere* nor love me save at our even-peril.

Remains

CLEVELAND – The mummified body of an Aborigine that had lain unclaimed for 109 years in the basement of a Cleveland funeral home was shipped back to Australia yesterday. The remains of Wanung will be buried next February in Queensland on the 110th anniversary of his death, a descendant, Walter Palm Island said. Wanung was one of nine Aborigines abducted from Palm and Hinchinbrook Islands in the early 1880s and forced to join a circus, where he was billed as Tambo Tambo, a 'ranting man-eater'. He died of pneumonia at 21 in a Cleveland hotel, and was embalmed and then forgotten until his body was turned over to the county coroner in August and she began an effort to send him home. – *Reuter*

(Toronto *Globe and Mail*, Thursday, December 9, 1993)

THE death and bestowal of Tambo Tambo was of insignificant moment in any secular scheme of things. Transported from Palm Island, he died in a side-street Cleveland hotel, of pneumonia, aged, at age twenty-one, fatally. With probably not one of his fellow exotic indigenes by his side.

For all surviving savages would have been, safely chained, demanded at the three gruelling evening performances, or the afternoon Matinée Gala Benefit for the Cleveland Widows and Orphans Fund; ranting black cannibals being, in the heart of darkest America, profitable to display.

Was there also taken naked, shuddering, from sun-drenched Palm Island with caged Tambo a ranting man-eating Ms Tambo, a nubile child to share in the New World throughout the long nights of our intemperate winters his bed in furtive ecstasy and howled bewilderment and a black despair

But the Show (despite inexorable death and iniquitous crippling taxes) of black ranting humans devouring one another, before we are all gone into the light that wells from the heart of things, even the human heart, the terrible show, as we all know, to the bone we know it, had to go on.

No: almost certainly, retching his purple guts up, his pink-frothed lungs coughed inside out, his crimsoned heart broken, black Tambo died alone. As we all do of course in our mortal disposition. Which is not, granted, a palatable truth steadfastly to entertain: but one that is widely known.

So, did the potted Ohio palms at the end of the lobby weep and wither into the brimming brass spittoons when the black news broke? Was rife lamentation permitted the sable kitchen-help? Did jet roaches firefangle down from the floral wallpaper to provide him cortège? Not on your life.

And meanwhile, back on basking Palm and Hinchinbrook Islands, did an unthrift sun cease at the instant of his death to shoot down vital gold on the spreading successive jasper perpetual waves and the rank green jungle-tangle? God only knows: such black rift being Immortal to behold.

Was there observed, for all of his long desiccated abeyance lying stacked at the back of a shelf in deep cupboard-blackness, even the faintest glow, some drifted tropical ocean-phosphorescence, to tell the funeral home's flunkeys they hoarded a precious relic, a dispossessed soul? In fact, no.

Might not some good-old-person, doffing his/her Grand Wizard's hood to slap on blackface, if told tonight of lost Tambo's inconsequent death, not pause appalled from death-rattling his/her tambourine in the First Gospel Church's basement at Ms Interlocutor? Don't hold your breath.

That Ohio coroner might have been welcomed at the Queensland burial of Tambo's mummified material remains. Not us. It is difficult indeed, to allow the bitter lives of one's kind, of one's sweet loves to pierce one: harder than being bereft of love, for many. Some nevertheless succeed.

Let us for what it is worth pray, that in his bright abduction Wanung saw his Blessed Island, come from forever's night, beckoned again in flame, in the living flame flared, close-cupped in the frosted rose fixture over his fouled cot and heard called in his mother tongue his original Name.

Philosopher
(for Peter)

That the daft marriage of body
and mind, that perennial chest-
nut, was morganatic, he knew.

His self-loathing was famous,
as misunderstood as his work
at its most gnomic. Wherein
he displayed (he had to employ
against intuition the witness
of language) to obdurate dons
and himself that the mind,
whatever in absent God's
terrible name that might prove
not to be, must be changed.

He made for himself, then,
a necessity of virtue: this
exacts a prodigious toll,
which he insisted can only
be paid in kind. He grasped
that egregious man must reason,
might even augur, lost causes;
and attempt to reckon the balance
of promise and *vanitas.*

Insufferably demanding,
he suffered fools not at all;
and was often on easy familiar
terms with the simple untutored.
After all-in bouts with the Thrones
of cerebration, drained, he liked
to sit through reruns of B movies;
he greatly admired Betty Hutton.

He was puzzled by Shakespeare,
admired Blake; and could not,
it would seem, credit a string
wound into a ball. But he made
of the threads he teased out,
with pious relentless attention
from the stuff of this world's
ragbag, marvellous motley
to cover the dour Emperor's
naked, shivering subjects;
painstakingly worked samplers
with stitched aphoristic texts
to be hung on the tatty last-
act canvas flats; hooked
prayer rugs with patterns
of convolute ramification
for the devotions of others.

Then let it be an accepted
article of a secular faith
in the evidence of fleet things
seen and sometimes shewn:
that after an ascetic's life
of self-imposed exile and self-
inflicted wounds, a life the which
he proclaimed '… wonderful',
he strode, erect and suspecting,
up through the dark gorges
of looming significance
into the burning ambush
(we needs must pray for him alway)
of understanding.

Remembering the Illecillewaet
and the Similkameen Rivers
(for Donald)

Setting forth once more, you gave what you had
to the weeping abandoned child on the bank
of the River Fuji. Bashō, that was not nothing.

Or not the nothing the bone-weary poet
may reckon loomed in the flamed evening,
a soft step falling bodiless beside him.

As on an oatmeal-glazed porcelain bowl
a single indigo swash may smoulder.

As one autumnal chrysanthemum blossom
becomes the season's bronze humdrum.

Poet, despite 'the irresistible will of heaven'
there is no bruised path ascending from Edo
to the summits of sun-drubbed clouds.

The sparrow, cocksure for your crumbs,
whets its merciless bird's beak and chirps
and chirps in the brilliant gutterglitter ah
longer flight ah weather-beaten death O
'bracelet of bright hair about the bone'. No.

No, love is not love which does not alter.
As you went to understand, past master,
steadfast as the green river descending,
boulder by broken boulder, to the moon's
heaved ocean, to the furrowed inland sea.

Syzygy

In his loneliness and fixedness he yearneth
The Emperor is always surrounded by

towards the journeying Moon,
a brilliant and yet ambiguous throng

and the stars that still sojourn, yet still move onward;
of nobles and courtiers – malice and enmity

and every where the blue sky belongs to them,
in the guise of servants and friends – who form

and is their appointed rest,
a counterweight ... to unseat

and their native country and their own natural homes,
the ruler from his place with poisoned arrows.

which they enter unannounced, as lords
The Empire is immortal, but the Emperor

that are certainly expected, and yet
himself totters and falls from

there is a silent joy at their arrival.
his throne, yes, whole dynasties

By the light of the Moon he beholdeth God's
sink in the end and breathe their last

creatures of the great calm.
in one death rattle.

The marginal glosses to *The Rime of the Ancient Mariner* were,
according to Ernest Hartley Coleridge, 'added in 1815–16, when a
collected edition of Coleridge's poems was being prepared for the
press, and were first published in Sibylline Leaves, 1817, but it is
possible that they were the work of a much earlier period.'

The passage from *The Great Wall of China* is from the
translation by Willa and Edwin Muir.

Articles of Faith
(for Alberto)

The passengers who ... numbered nine hundred, were then quartered for
the most part in a camp at Aïn-Seba, on the outskirts of Çasablanca.
They were there for seventeen days. In two large halls they slept on the
cement floor, wrapped in their blankets.... She wrote from morning to
night, monopolizing one of the camp's few chairs in order to do this.
When she had to leave her chair, her mother or father sat down on it to
hold it for her. In the morning they would rise before everyone else and
at night they would go to bed last – all because of the chair. People were
amazed and asked her parents. 'What does your daughter do? Is she a
journalist?' She was in fact writing commentaries on the Pythagorean
text that form the last part of *Intuitions préchrétiennes* ...

Simone Pétrement, *Simone Weil: A Life*, trans. Raymond Rosenthal
(New York: Pantheon, 1976), p. 469

And if we do not understand
(I say I do not understand)
the complete implication of
Simone Weil's commandeered chair,
we are, I believe, forgiven:
for '... the universe is not only
queerer than we suppose, but
queerer than we *can* suppose ...'

I see it, a hand-me-down discard
from somebody's uncle's kitchen,
its coats of cheap broccoli-green
paint chipped from manhandling,
its splayed legs wonky, its wooden
seat smoothed like old seastones
by homespun backsides, its knurled

rungs scuffed bare by hobnails,
a battered straight-backed wreck
redeemed forever, a scholar's chair
in the camp's sacramental carrel.

(But not a collapsed, collapsing
contraption like Glenn Gould's low-
slung seat, creaking in ecstasy,
held together with stove-pipe wire.

I have handled that chair, under
his fretful direction; and brought
bowls of almost-scalding water
in which he would soak his hands,
there were only two by my count,
before a performance. And reckon
myself honoured beyond reason.)

I see it placed in the hazed sun,
a trash throne in the turmoil
of sick apprehensions and hopes,
surrounded by bickering dons:
Idealists; Realists; some who know
the Lion of sanctuary, and that
this chair must be always about
in the ivy-clad quad, and some
gifted philosophers, versed
in the plaiting of hairs, who do not.

And surrounded by numinous hosts:
rejoicing, exultant, triumphant
Cherubim, Seraphim, Thrones;

and the savants of classic Athens
who discounted women and slaves;
and mullahs and priests and parsons
and rabbis, all beaten senseless;
and black-jackbooted Nazis. They
are not (yet) on speaking terms.

And should we not understand
(I say that you do understand)
the dear import of Simone Weil's
commandeered chair in her kin's
jealous keeping, then good sir,
we are not, I also believe, liable
to find forgiveness in this world:

and the Fat Lady will not sing
and Christ is not risen and
the Holocaust which is not
over will never be over.

Two Maritime Poems

In memory of Amy Clampitt
'… a lighthouse, light-
pierced like a needle's eye'

Garbage In, Garbage Out
(Bay of Fundy)

One wave succeeds another.
Each is of honed grey steel.
That light is flashing artifice;
its jagged rock is real,

where vessels may be riven.
In brute fact many have.
This livid purple bottle
that held a brand of salve

is bobbing in a tangle
of yellow polythene.
We cast about for flotsam,
who are at heart marine,

that might escape attention.
The ocean will not halt.
Whales sunder the horizon.
Man does much by default.

Stared Down

Man having been removed from the light,
    this giant occulted blinding eye
    (that once burned sperm whale oil)

    blinks back at the steady horizon-line
    across this bland afternoon untended
by any keeper. No more nimble scrabble

    of piebald goats on the basalt outcrop,
    no kempt green oblong of garden patch
    in the lee of the regular white house,

no occasional smoke ripped from the twin
    chimneys, no motley laundry cracked
    like mad flags to spell out habitation.

And no more human error. Nor fatal nor
    (for man betimes has mistaken an azure
Heaven) redemptive. We are still warned

    as we must be, given our dispositions,
    of jagged hazard; assured of an exact
    location in plunged night: and besides

on a clear day like this you can see forever.

Three for Sneaky Pete

Rites

It is not Christ the Tiger:
now molten in gold scrub,
now instant crossing before the raked moon:
Single and Killer.

It is not Christ the Lamb:
tipsy, bloodfleeced bright inches above
the swirled-emerald turf of Beulah:
Abundant, Victim.

It is not Christ the Goat:
omnivorous, rank, opaline-eyed,
quick on precarious tips, randy as old Pan,
Wicked to butt Eve.

It is not Christ our Redeemer.
Standing ever just over the swift river
in fireshadow in lightblaze demanding
Identity Himself.

O it is O nevertheless poor *Christ!*
as plausible, suave, articulate
Gent in his own semblance
stricken with recognition:

Good Citizen first and foremost
of no fixed address, Who ponders recall
as the certain temper of metals,
as the bourse-price of electrum:

––––

and Bridegroom and Guest and Best Man
caught up in the brash squalor, the shrill-squealed
abandon of obsolete instruments, indecorous
during the nuptials and long after.

Ascension
(From *The Hunterian Psalter*, c. 1170)

Tennyson could, and did,
rhyme us 'faith' with 'death'.
Winters, cunningly enough,
has offered us 'Nazareth'.
Most poets nowadays prefer
to save their mortal breath.

We are only shown of Christ
his elegant unmarked feet
below a gold-hemmed white
robe, not a winding-sheet,
borne up on the spread wings
of two angels the Paraclete

has uttered for His ascent.
Each, neither old nor young,
displays an anguine scroll
with words in a dead tongue:
'viri' and so forth, written
in crimson script. Among

the Apostles, much stylized,
who gesticulate and gawk
upwards in pure wonderment
is Mary, who found the rock
rolled from the tomb's mouth.
Her hands, in lovely shock

raised, palms outwards turned,
prefigure the angels' wings.
Heaven enfolding Him is shown
as wavered concentric rings
of blue and ochre and pale green
and beige. Among other things,

Voyager 2 has sent back
in redundant prolonged trice
a similar image (enhanced)
of the antique water ice
that orbits Saturn: such is
our either/or's device.

From a Flemish Diptych

They are gathered in adoration under three foliate ogives:
two standing, their left hands gesturing heavenwards,
the third, in profile, kneeling to tender his offering.

The elaborate flow of the fall of their robes is the work
of a master, composed and enfolded; he has chosen to carve,
in the sensuous texture of yellowing ivory, Mary's mantle
one with the Infant's full-skirted garment, enveloping them.

Herod is not depicted. Of course he is present at every
Nativity. This has not changed since the fourteenth century;
or the first. All artists assume it that they may continue

to shew with such loving exact detail the impotent Christ-
child with his Mother, serene and smiling, as if nothing
else in the world has mattered, before or since this bestowal.

In Memory of Northrop Frye

Perhaps back to the hinterlands, to the clear cold springs
that reflect everything but his image, from which rivers rise.
Perhaps to the slopes of mountains, to which he could say
with complete assurance: 'Remove hence to yonder place ...'
Perhaps to the swept meadows of perfect minuscule flowers
and thousand-year-old shrubs. Not to the barren peaks.

He was known along the coast where, as he would have insisted,
he was only '... finding a smoother pebble or a prettier shell';
and at the deltas of tawny rivers where dugouts are clustered
he could be found in familiar discourse with the natives,
who trusted him. He would not be revered. And spent long hours
scrutinizing the great ocean all undiscovered before him.

When he departed, he left behind him elaborate maps of *Terra
Incognita;* the rudiments of a grammar; a code broken open;
a *Sailing Instructions* for mariners that, if many will perish
in the destructive element immersed, some lives may be saved.
These survive him, his graceful anatomies. He was much loved.

We could mourn him. But that would be boasting.

Reflections from a Dark Glass

Graveyard

Fenced off from fall wheat where
two township roads are crossed,
a quarter-acre square
chock-full of local stones;
some toppled by hard frost,
strewn like giants' bones.

Whoever set the board
upon this cluttered ground
must have unearthed a hoard
of pieces like the morse
antique chessmen found
on Lewis, for perforce,

to strike the souls of those
whom they commemorate
in staggered serried rows,
no two are carved the same.
Now common in their fate,
the dead do not lay blame

for darker disarray,
nor that they came to lose
the game they had to play,
constrained on every hand
by rules they did not choose
and do not understand.

Diorama

Children are filed past
the curved, glass-fronted stage:
the monstrous *Odonata* rest,
blaze-winged, in an age

labelled prehistoric.
And may continue where
all that will persist of us
is the glitter-stare

of beings who consider
a hyper-space relief,
our reconstructed likeness,
in crystal disbelief.

My love, no matter. Nothing,
not even you and I,
in our rare demonstration
must or cannot die.

Long Shots

Langland, a garbage-person for going on now
nearly seventeen years, has yet to discover
a single chucked-out ruby-incrusted tiara.
But given his stolid conservative convictions,
keeps looking. Where there's hope there's death.

After a long mad night at the ivory eye-piece,
the Royal Astronomer called it another day.
Before retiring, he fudged his notes, trusting
that no one would notice in his lifetime:
God, he reminded himself, does not advertise.

At the heart of the rotting heart of the fallen
man he digested the fact: that in good time,
prized for his swallow-tailed scalloped turquoise
and brass-green wings with golden symmetrical
mock eyes, he would thrash in a killing-bottle.

He told the Truth to the Courtesan on his left,
murmuring, 'Pass it on ...', hoping against hope
that by the time it had been bobbled around
the brilliant gregarious circle it might return,
discreetly, with the port, believable at last.

Long Weekend at the Lake
(for A.M.D.)

We wait in vain for fate
in samite guise
to raise from the face of the lake
the perilous great
burnished blade: of late

she does not deign to appear;
not given cause.
And how shall love profit where
no knight attends
lady or liege lord? Here

dawn is a lifted clenched
fist of light,
noon's wound not stanched,
each nightfall
a red rage quenched.

Where allot blame, that we lack
deliverance? Not
to nature of course, nor sweet luck;
not to God,
nor ourselves: but overhead, back

in the City, stars will duel
to bright death,
and a pocked wafer spill
quicksilver
to phosphor a neighbours' pool.

Brief Homily and Homage

And I thought: Keep calm Pompey, think of the little birds.
And at that, up came a moorhen and bit a swan on the backside.

Stevie Smith, *Novel on Yellow Paper*

Crow, cock-of-the-mound!
It writhes with worms;
they are full of it.
The world will wound
us with false alarums.
No denying that.

Cock, crow in the elm,
an interested eye
shiny beady black
on the lost lamb.
It won't last the day
and that's a fact.

Flock, birds of a feather!
Rise, 'a fling of seed'
fall in least death
to earth, by our Father
accounted it is said:
and that's the Truth.

Icarus fell ablaze
in a silent scream
to the heaved sea.
Which without pause
closed over him.
That's what they say.

O Falcon hung
in kindled flame!
Chevalier!
Caught daylong
in light's flume!
That's as may be ...

Glenn's Riffs

Sweet vertigo, I love you!
The counterpoint of dread,
a labyrinth below me;
and high above my head

the ecstasies of giants,
gods' blood on their hands,
basso in their innards.
No man understands,

who has not once been frozen,
transfixed by fear because
he overhears himself ascend
a descant of applause.

Back off, Jack! I've been there:
nailed, root and firecrown,
halfway up your green beanstalk,
halfway down.

The Flight out of Egypt

I will tell you a story. Or I will not
tell you a story. That once upon a time
I tried to respond in kind to the mute universe.

Here was the ocean fumbled at endless length
over the rocks. The world will come to an end,
of course. There is hope, said Kafka; but not for us.

One distant intricate ship sank with the sun,
quenched, with all souls presumably lost. Or we
did not find them the following morning with the usual

resurrection of fire, of stained flame spread
along the fine-crimped wire of the horizon. No,
though the sun rose, bearer of tales of other fire.

II

In the absence, not of God, but of the prophetic,
with Phoenix ash, pumice-fine, everywhere sifted,
it became our very onus to harrow our whereabouts.

But outline was lost. Mass, massive, massy,
the oceans rolled, heaved with a sick slick
onto the vague land, so far and no further,

withdrew as usual, leaving its wrack-lines
of interwoven foreboding staining the formerly
gold sand. We bowed, but translation escaped us

until, inland, beyond the slashed rain forest,
the insatiable fire-fledgling screamed again and again
with primitive rage. Once, once was enough.

III

To tell you of death. At full noon the youth,
all of his father's promise, his mother's grief,
fell like a fleshstone down from the topmast

crosstree, plunged through the hatched shrouds,
the necessary rigging, the parti-coloured sails
to smash on the seamed deck. Parlous, a sudden

vast fist had canted our vessel, nearly careened
us in mid-ocean, here, halfway from there to there.
Caught unawares, still staggered, aghast, we stared

in dumb conjecture at the unbelievable bright blood
slow-spread on the commonplace holystoned planks:
an antipodal sun continued elsewhere to rise and set.

IV

As we say. Once, in choosing a sacramental stone,
one of the burnished plenitude strewn at my feet,
I threw it as far as I might out into the hugely

indifferent ocean. At once the barely discernible
rings started to spread outward. Love, it is this,
when they reach the rare bound of the universe of words

(we have contrived just such stringent myths
in fictions sans gods or beasts or withered heroes
or mazarined maidens or bloodwine or sacred leaven

or the least promise of valour), becomes my prayer:
that they will in the new-sanctioned order of things
curve and return upon us shrived in this telling.

Dove Legend

I batter upward
spiral to lightblaze in rare air &

my marvellous chambered heart
lest it bloodburst falls

a crimson fleck a vermilion iota
unnoticed down & down & down

through the pillared fire of mansioned clouds
brightwoven from all horizon & far

below my marvellous heart settles
at last to rest in the plundered breast-

feathered nest of a vivid resplendent quetzal.
Soon looted by feral urchins, it may be seen,

set as a blood ruby & reckoned priceless,
in the nit-infested, flamingo-pink silk

turban of one of the lesser steadfast
Prophets of mundane doom,

by some who have eyes to see still
marvellous still beating.

Contents

PART III

Abstract Memoir

PART IV

Tradecraft

Index of First Lines of Poems

Richard Outram is a graduate of the University of Toronto (English and Philosophy) and is now retired from the Canadian Broadcasting Corporation. He is the author of numerous collections of poetry including *Man in Love* (1985), *Hiram and Jenny* (1988) and *Mogul Recollected* (1993), all published by The Porcupine's Quill. His latest collection, *Benedict Abroad*, won the City of Toronto Book Award for 1999.

Outram's work has also been published in many journals and magazines in Canada, the United States and Britain. He has given numerous public readings, including appearances at the Harbourfront Reading Series and at the National Library of Canada.

Outram is married to painter and wood engraver Barbara Howard; together they have produced many fine books and broadsides under their own Gauntlet Press imprint.

Critic Alberto Manguel has described Richard Outram as 'one of the finest poets in the English language'.